D0744290

Gem Cutting Is Easy

BY

MARTIN WALTER

All photographs by Joe Rothstein

CROWN PUBLISHERS, INC.
New York

To Marga

© 1972 by Martin Walter

Library of Congress Catalog Card Number: 72-84318

ISBN: 0-517-500205
ISBN: 0-517-500213

Printed in the United States of America
Published simultaneously in Canada by
General Publishing Company Limited
Designed by Ruth Smerechniak

Contents

Equipment

GEM CUTTING HAS A HISTORY probably just a little less ancient than the history of homo sapiens. Fine examples of extremely skilled lapidary work are known to us which can be reliably dated anywhere from six to seven thousand years ago. Finds in Olduvai Gorge prove that man worked with stone a half-million years ago. Until very recently, gem cutting was a closely held family secret. As a hobby practiced by amateurs, it is only a few decades old. The number of cutters is, however, increasing by leaps and bounds and would probably grow even faster if more people realized how easy it is to get started, how fundamentally simple are procedures, and how much satisfaction can be derived from the hobby.

How to Start

There are hundreds of thousands of potential cutters in the United States who are held back from enjoying a wonderful hobby by not knowing how to start. I know this from my own experience and that of many friends as well as by answering countless telephone calls to the Lapidary and Gem Society of New York, by people who are in that situation.

To my mind, the easiest way to start is to obtain a copy of the *Rockhound Buyers' Guide*, which is the April number of *Lapidary Journal*. It can be obtained by writing to the Lapidary Journal, P.O. Box 2369, San Diego, California 92112. A check or money order for $1.75 should be enclosed. It lists all dealers in lapidary supplies and equipment in the U.S.A. In addition to carrying their ads, it contains a listing of all mineral clubs. Pick a club in your area, call the secretary, and attend the next meeting of the club. While there, ask questions. If no club is close to you, visit the nearest dealer.

Rockhounds are a friendly crowd and like to make converts.

Find out whether there is lapidary instruction available in your town or city. Dealers will know. This is the easiest way to learn.

If there is no instruction available, the art can be learned by reading a book or books. If this is the way you intend to go about it, do not read the first chapter and then rush to buy equipment. Go through the whole book, even though some of the contents at first may mystify you. Do not get discouraged, even though everything is not clear on first reading. There is nothing to gem cutting that anyone with average intelligence cannot master with ease. Having taught a great many beginners over many years as instructor at the Craft Students League in New York City, I cannot remember a single case when a pupil did not cut his or her first stone in the first three-hour lesson. An instructor will naturally speed things up, but even without one, no great difficulties will be encountered.

What to Acquire in the Way of Machinery

When first buying machinery for your lapidary work, you are probably not sure how deeply you will want to involve yourself. You also are bound to be confused by the multitude of choices. I therefore strongly recommend you start with one of the small multipurpose machines that come ready to use, with necessary accessories except the motor, a ¼-h.p. electric motor that must be bought separately. B and I Manufacturing Company was the first to offer such a unit, but other similar apparatus has since come into the market. The B and I machine has a simple sleeve bearing, which eventually will wear out, but is fairly easy to replace. Others of the same kind come with ball bearings that last a much longer time, but are naturally more expensive. A unit that comes with all equipment is, of course, a boon to the beginner. The obvious disadvantage of such a tool is that for each operation one has to change the working part. Should you find that gem cutting is a lasting hobby, you can acquire additional machinery. In that case you can use the B and I or equivalent as auxiliary equipment; for example, you can leave it permanently set up as a polisher or use it as a faceting unit.

When you are ready to go in for heavier equipment, you have a choice of combination machinery, where grinders, sanders, polishing discs, and in some cases a saw are all operating on one shaft, or regular double arbors that swing two stones or sanding drums, one on each side of the bearing. The combination machines are preferable if you have limited space. If, however, you have room, the double arbor is much more practical when it comes to changing the working parts. As often happens the most expensive turns out in the long run to be the cheapest. Should you decide to buy a combination unit, buy one that has three speeds. Do not buy a unit on which the saw is connected to the same shaft with the rest of the wheels. The combination units come fully equipped with grinding stones. For the arbors, all accessories

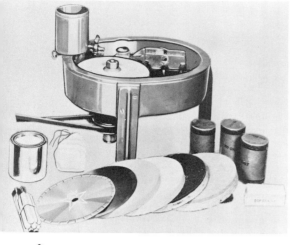

Illustrated here is the B and I machine. A larger version is also available. Both machines come with the additional equipment shown.

A combination machine has facilities for all operations, from grinding to sanding to polishing, on one unit. *Photo, Highland Park Mfg.*

Combination machines are also available in table models.
Photo, Highland Park Mfg.

have to be purchased separately. In that case, either two or three double arbors would be required. One would be mounted with a grinding stone on each end, the other with a sanding drum on one side and polishing equipment on the other. The ideal setup would be three double arbors, one for grinding, one for polishing, and one for sanding. This would make it possible to accomplish each operation at optimum speed with a minimum of contaminating the polishing equipment by rough particles from the grinding operation.

Grindstones come in different grit sizes. These grits are held together by a ceramic bond that also comes in different hardnesses. The harder the bond, the longer the wheel will last, but the slower its cutting action will be. The hardness is expressed by letters, K being harder than L, L harder than M. The finer the grit the slower the cut, but the better the surface on the cut gem.

Grinding wheels come in various grits and bond.

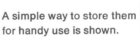

A simple way to store them for handy use is shown.

For our purposes, 320 and 220 grit are best. Grit sizes are given in figures expressing the number of imaginary holes per square inch in a sieve that would produce so fine a powder. The more holes, the finer the powder. A good size grinding stone to use is 1½ to 2 inches wide by 8-inch diameter. The arbor hole is chosen according to the size of the shaft you selected (either ¾ or one inch). Most wheels are manufactured with a lead bushing (lining of the hole). The larger the wheels used, the larger should be the shaft they swing on.

Sanding can be done either on sanding discs or sanding drums. Sanding discs are slightly convex metal plates, covered with fairly hard foam rubber on which a disc of sanding cloth is fastened. They come from the manufacturer with the rubber covered with thin canvas material to which the sanding cloth is glued. For polishing, similar discs covered with leather are furnished. It is a good idea to use these leather-covered discs to carry the sanding cloth, too, since the canvas deteriorates fast and comes off with pieces of the rubber cushioning when changing of sanding equipment becomes necessary.

Sanding drums come in two varieties. On one, strips of sanding cloth are held by means of a split screw. On the other, more recent version the sanding cloth is in the form of an endless belt, held in place by the expansion of a layer of rubber, which takes place as the wheel revolves. This is the more desirable arrangement, since it permits fast changes.

Leather and cloth or canvas belts are available for these expansion drums which can be used for polishing. Polishing can also be done on slightly convex discs on which a leather covering is stretched. The manufacturers furnish these discs ready for use.

A saw is furnished with a B and I type machine. It is awkward to handle, but usable. If possible, a small trim saw should be added to

A sanding disc is glued to a leather polishing disc.

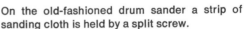

On the old-fashioned drum sander a strip of sanding cloth is held by a split screw.

On the expanding drum sander an endless sanding belt is held by expansion of a rubber cushion, which takes place when in motion.

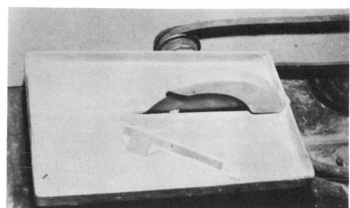

A small, inexpensive model saw is good to have. It can be mounted with a 6-inch blade or very thin 4- or 5-inch blade for sawing expensive material, as shown here.

the equipment. Inexpensive machines of this type are on the market. These can be used at first as regular trim saws and later on, when more equipment is added, set with a thin bronze blade to cut faceting or other expensive rough (gem material in its natural state) only.

Also needed are the following items:

1. An aluminum pencil. This can be purchased in any variety store in the form of knitting needles. The thinnest purchasable are just right. The point can be sharpened on the same grinding wheels we use for gem cutting.

2. An alcohol lamp. It is a good idea to replace the standard wick with a homemade one of candlewicking. This is used by plumbers and is available at all hardware stores. Fuel for the same. A quart of

Accessory equipment, which is needed at the start, includes a thin aluminum knitting needle, a pocket-knife, a ceramic tile, a pair of tweezers, a small gauge marked with inches and centimeters, and a wrench.

An alcohol lamp is needed to heat dopping wax, stones, and dops. Shown is a ball of candlewicking and a homemade wick.

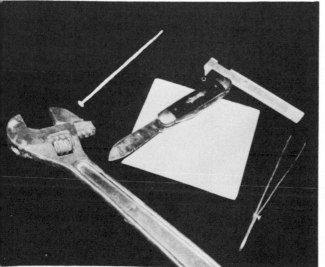

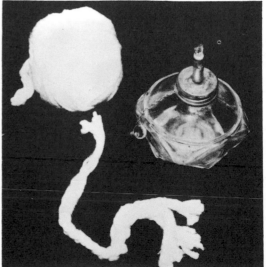

alcohol goes a long way if the lamp is extinguished regularly when not in use and the cap that comes with every lamp is put on religiously when the lamp is not in use.

3. A small jar with tight cover for alcohol in which to wash stones free of dopping wax.

4. A ceramic tile or a piece of marble from an old tabletop or a discarded pen base of onyx or glass to be used in shaping the hot dopping wax.

5. A large pair of tweezers.

6. A caliper marked with both inches and millimeters. (This is useful but not absolutely necessary.)

7. A set of templates made of plastic or metal.

8. An old pocket knife.

9. A wrench to tighten lock nuts.

In addition, we will need some polishing and cutting compounds. Most of these are inexpensive and can be bought by the pound.

For polishing powders we should have tin oxide and cerium oxide. Also good to have are tripoli, which is used for prepolishing, and chromium oxide, which helps in polishing some of the problem stones. Linde A powder is more expensive, but it sometimes achieves a polish when nothing else will, and two ounces will go a long way.

Silicon-carbide powders in grades of 220 and 600 are often needed.

The best way to store abrasive and polishing powders is to buy a dozen mason jars, preferably quart size, and keep them in the original box. By reversing the lids in the covers, so that the white enamel is uppermost, it is possible to mark the contents with a marking pen. Keep a plastic spoon of the kind used for picnics in each jar. If a label is affixed to glass, cover it with clear nail polish or transparent Scotch tape. Of course, the old trick of fastening the cover to the underside of a shelf can also be used, particularly if such a shelf is handy to the place of use, then simply screw the jars into the fastened tops.

New ways of applying polishing and fine abrasive powders have recently come into use. One is a material called Pellon, which is sold in discs with adhesive backing. Its use will be explained more extensively later on. The newest wrinkle in polishing is a wafer-thin plastic material impregnated with various cutting and polishing agents. It is called Ultralap and is manufactured by Pfizer Minerals, Pigments and Metal Division. According to their claims, it may be used for polishing cabochons and faceted stones. It is a little more expensive to use than standard methods. Where stones may be polished easily by traditional procedures, it is therefore not economical. But there are many applica-

Mason jars make fine containers for storing polishing and abrasive powders.

tions where Ultralap will produce a polish when practically nothing else will, as, for example, in the case of faceting fluorite and apatite. There are other instances where there is a choice between Ultralap and diamond compounds, in which case Ultralap may be just as, or less, costly in the working of peridot, garnet, and tourmaline. Here is a fertile field for experimentation.

New Diamond Products

While powdered diamond has long been used, particularly to cut diamonds and also to impregnate faceting laps, it has, since the introduction of the synthetic diamond, become available in a wide range of sizes.

The synthetic diamond products manufactured by the General Electric Company are a great boon to the cutter, particularly the faceter. Many problem stones can now be polished with ease. Tables (the flat top surfaces of faceted gemstones) can be polished on wood impregnated with 8000 and 12000 mesh either mixed with oil or the commercial mixtures that are sold in plastic syringes. Facets can be polished on well-scored Lucite or similar plastics with the diamond mixtures.

The harder stones, topaz and corundum, polish well on tin impregnated with diamond. If the facets are small it is usually unnecessary to employ a coolant since little heat is generated. Where a coolant is needed, the diamond compound should be applied to the inner parts of the lap (the horizontal disc used for polishing) with the coolant dripping close to the periphery. By moving the stone over the entire surface, the stone is cooled without the compound's being washed off the lap.

Another saving of diamond powder can be effected by collecting the diamond scraped off the lap and adhering to the stone being polished. Collect it on a small scrap of material or leather and reapply it to the lap when needed.

Diamond powders come in many grades, which may be designated either in mesh sizes or microns. Mesh sizes are based on the number of holes in a square inch of an imaginary sieve through which particles of the powder would pass. A micron is 1/1000 of a millimeter. These grades apply to diamond products as well as to other grinding and polishing powders. The following is a comparison table giving both microns and mesh sizes:

Micron	Mesh
¼	100,000
½	60,000
1	14,000
3	8,000
6	3,000
9	1,800
15	1,200
30	600
45	325
60	230

A transparent refrigerator dish with airtight cover protects loupes from dust.

A double loupe attached to a headband helps greatly in doing exacting work.

Other Auxiliary Equipment

The following items are not absolute necessities, but add to the quality of the work performed. The most important of these is some form of magnifying glass or loupe. Most households have one of these. A jeweler's eye loupe is desirable. A good way to keep loupes in a usually dusty lapidary shop is in a clear plastic refrigerator jar with tight-fitting cover. A headband loupe is a great comfort while faceting, because it is always there, yet does not get in the way.

Plastic bags, sold in food stores, are a fine protection against damage and contamination for laps of all kinds. Pigeonhole sections from an old desk are handy for storing laps.

Last, but not the least useful item on this list, is a dust mask, which can be bought at any good hardware or paint store. It should be worn when doing a lot of dry sanding to avoid inhaling the resulting dust.

Don't rush into purchasing too many things at one time because often odds and ends around the house can be used as we go along. Gem cutting does not have to be an expensive hobby. Motors of discarded washing machines often have a long life left. Wooden discs, which were supposed to be lamp bases but which can be used for laps, are often found in surplus stores for pennies. Lucite and Plexiglas can be found in the same stores for a fraction of the cost of ready-made discs if one is willing to use a jigsaw to cut them out. Scrap leather

Pigeonholes from old desks are good storage places for laps.

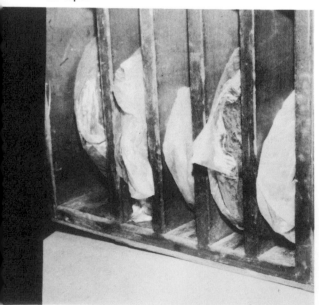

A dust mask protects your health.

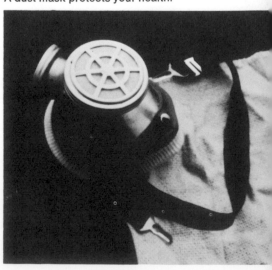

costs practically nothing. As will be pointed out later, it is possible to make one's own diamond laps. The owner of a lathe is, of course, at a great advantage as he can true his own laps. Old felt hats and scraps of new carpet may also be turned into polishing discs.

The Care and Feeding of Lapidary Machinery

Most books on lapidary instruction seem to assume that the future gem cutter is an accomplished machinist. Since I have not found this to be so in the case of myself and most of my pupils, let me give here some pointers on the maintenance of lapidary machinery.

The motive power for lapidary machines is supplied by electric motors, which come in different sizes graded according to power output. The sizes we use most frequently are ¼, ⅓, and ½ horsepower. The larger the motor, the more power it consumes, but the less chance there is of its being overworked and overheated.

An electric motor, which has little holes on each end above the bearings, should be oiled at intervals.

Motors are manufactured to work on alternating current or direct current. Modern buildings practically all have alternating current. Motors are made to work on regular house current—110 volt in most places, and 220 volt. A 220-volt motor requires special wire installation but is preferable. The wiring to which the motor is connected should be large enough and the fuse ample. If the lights in the room dim when you switch on the motor, the circuit is overloaded and an electrician should be consulted. If too small, the wires may heat up enough to start a fire when you work for a long time. If an electrician makes your installation, he will provide you with a three-pronged outlet that eliminates the danger of electrical shock.

Motors come with sleeve bearings and ball bearings, and the most expensive even have sealed bearings (the lubrication is sealed in). If there are little holes on each end of the motor, the motor should be lubricated with light motor oil. This should be done in moderation, since too much oil is just as bad as not enough. If the motor works for a long time without getting too hot to touch, it is working properly. A motor should be cleaned regularly. Blowing out lint from inside the motor can be done by attaching a vacuum cleaner hose to the wrong end of the machine, thus turning it into a blower. The stuff blown out of the motor is usually pretty messy, so make provisions to catch it where it won't do any harm.

Motors come with single and double shafts. The single-shaft model can pull only one appliance, while the double shaft (one sticking out at each end) can be used to work two appliances simultaneously.

Motors are usually connected to lapidary machinery by V-belts (endless rubber belts of triangular profile), which run on grooved wheels called pulleys. These pulleys are attached to the shaft of the motor or appliance by a set screw. If the shafts are flattened on one side, the set screw should clamp down on this side. These pulleys are available at all good hardware stores in several sizes with different size arbor holes. It is, therefore, important to know the size of the motor shaft and the size of the shaft that carries the grinding implements when purchasing pulleys. There are also sets of three pulleys of different size available.

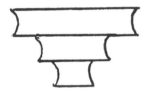

A profile of two triple pulleys mounted opposite each other.

These triple pulleys are mounted in such a manner that the largest diameter of the motor pulley is opposite the smallest size pulley on the tool.

Most of our machinery is furnished complete with pulleys, but you may occasionally wish to change the existing arrangement. It is important to remember that most motors revolve 1,750 times a minute. If pulleys on the motor and the tool are of the same size, both revolve at the same speed. If the motor pulley is twice the size of the tool pulley, the tool will revolve at twice the speed of the motor; if half the size, it will revolve at half the speed. To make it easier to change

Shown here are the three arrangements of the belt on triple pulleys. From left to right: slow, medium (or motor) speed, and fast.

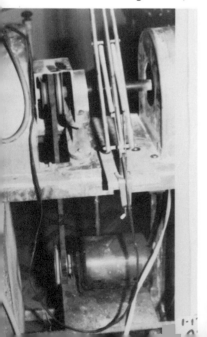  

The motor here is mounted on a commercial "floating rail." The weight of the motor holds the belt in tension.

speed on multiple pulley arrangements, it is good to be able to move the motor. This can be arranged by mounting the motor on a board with a slot or slots through which a large bolt runs, with a wing nut, if possible, and washer arrangement that makes it possible to fasten the board in any desired position. There also exist commercial fasteners that hold the motor on one side only, the other being held down by the weight of the motor.

All machinery that revolves has a turning shaft, which in turn is held in place by bearings. These may be just holes in a piece of steel, or they may be lined to reduce friction with rollers or balls (roller or ball bearings), or with a steel sleeve to make it possible to replace the hole in which the shaft runs without replacing the whole tool (sleeve bearings). Some bearings have sealed-in lubrication—others have to be lubricated. This is done with either grease or oil. If your machinery has small holes with or without cover, it expects to be oiled. If it is equipped with something that looks like a large, straight-sided thimble, it expects to be greased.

The grease cup arrangement on a B and I machine.

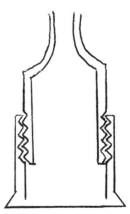

A profile cut through a grease cup.

Cup grease is smeared on the inside of this attachment, which is then replaced on the opening and screwed down as hard as possible. This will force the grease into the parts to be lubricated. If the machinery has some attachments sticking out that look like small spigots, grease has to be forced into them with a grease gun.

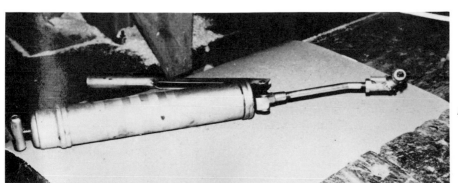

A grease gun.

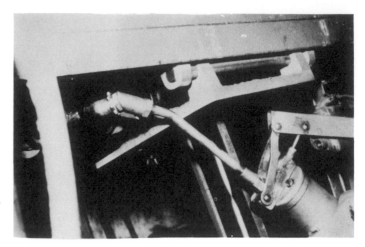

A grease gun in use.

Cutting wheels will eventually deform. They then have to be dressed. This can be done with a commercial wheel dresser used in machine shops: it consists of a cast-iron handle in which are mounted freely revolving wheels of hard steel. This instrument is rested on a tool rest, which comes with all cutting arbors, and is slowly pushed

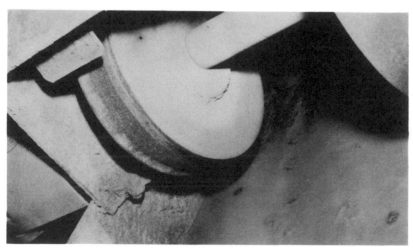

Shown here is a badly deformed wheel in need of "dressing."

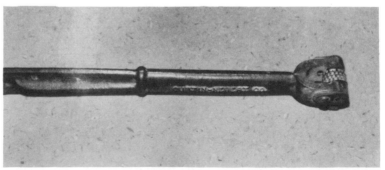

A commercial wheel dresser.

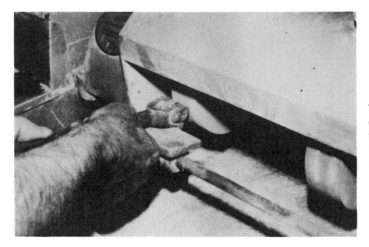

The wheel dresser rests on a tool rest, barely touching the highest point of the grinding wheel.

into the revolving wheel until the wheels on the dresser touch the grinding stones. They will revolve rapidly and in doing so grind away the high spots of the stone. This is a noisy and exciting operation, which often splinters the edges of the wheels because lapidary wheels are made with a much softer bond than the grinding stones used for steel tools.

A slower but more refined method, resulting in a better cutting surface, is the use of a diamond wheel dresser. This is a rod of tool steel into whose point a diamond is set. These are, of course, much more expensive but last a long time if used correctly. The tool again is rested on a tool rest so that the diamond touches the wheel's rim just below its center.

Be sure that only the diamond touches the grinding stone because if the metal holding it is ground away, the diamond will be knocked off. It will be hard to retrieve and even harder to find someone to set it back in place. Move the diamond point back and forth slowly, keeping it in the same plane, starting on the points of the wheel which stick

Diamond wheel dressers come set with one piece of diamond or with many small diamond chips. The one-stone dresser is really all that is needed. The multiple-diamond dresser is good for producing a really smooth surface.

out most—usually the rims. Keep the water running, since this keeps dust down, and check the effects of your efforts at frequent intervals by stopping the motor and revolving it slowly by hand. The low spots will show in a different color. Dressing has to go on until the wheel is completely round. Highland Park manufactures a diamond wheel

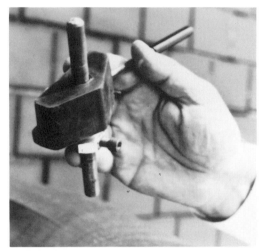

A jig to hold the diamond dresser is of great help.

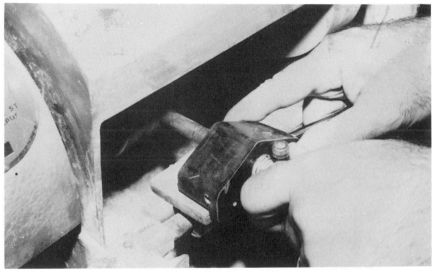

The diamond dresser is applied either held by hand or in jig, resting on tool rest. The diamond or diamonds should touch the grinding wheel just below an imaginary horizontal line drawn through its center.

dresser set with seven small diamonds rather than one larger one. This is very useful in smoothing out a wheel surface after it has been dressed generally. They also furnish a jig to hold either kind of diamond dresser, which greatly facilitates the operation of dressing a wheel. Dressing wheels is time consuming and should be kept to a minimum. High cutting speeds will reduce the need for it. Getting used to moving the work will also help. Grinding very large pieces of rough deforms wheels badly. Occasionally an expert lapidary will deform a wheel for certain purposes, but the beginner will do much better work on wheels that are true.

Maintenance of Combination Machines

Combination machines usually come with a leather disc for polishing on one end and on the other, a cloth-covered disc to which sanding discs are cemented. They have, in addition, a sanding drum and two cutting wheels. We have found that in replacing the sanding discs, the cloth covering soon gives way. We are, therefore, using leather covered discs to carry the sanding cloth. The same applies for the polishing discs. It is a major operation to replace the leather covering when it is worn through. We therefore now glue a leather disc to the original covering. It will then be only a simple glue job when the leather cover needs replacement.

When the cloth on the sanding drums wears out, do not try to replace it while leaving the drum on the machine. It is easy to remove the sanding drum by loosening the Allen set screw with the tool that is furnished with the machine, after first taking off the wheel guard and the disc mounted on the end of the axle. There is a hexagonal nut on one side. Lay the drum down with this side on top, loosen the nut, and turn the slotted screw that it held in place, so that the slot is at right angles to the rim. This will make it easy to pull off the old sanding cloth. Use this as a pattern to cut a new cover. Put it in place of the old one, pulling the end through the screw slot as tightly as possible. Then, using a screwdriver, turn the screw as far as possible. This will tighten the cloth still more; then fasten the screw in place with the holding nut.

The real difficulty occurs when the grinding wheels have to be replaced:

Step One: Remove the cover from the machine by loosening the screws and wing bolts that hold it in place.

Step Two: Remove the polishing disc and sanding drum.

Step Three: Remove the guard covering the bearing next to the sanding drum. Trace a line around the base of the bearing with the screwdriver in order to be able to replace it exactly as it was.

Step Four: Loosen the nut slightly that holds the grinding wheels in place. Before you do that, remove with an old nailbrush all the grit that has accumulated on the thread. It may be necessary to tap it lightly and use some oil on it.

Step Five: Loosen the screws that hold down the base of the bearing. Loosen the Allen set screws that hold the bearing to the shaft. Push the bearing off the shaft.

Step Six: Remove the nut that holds the grinding wheels in place.

Step Seven: Take the belt off the pulleys. Remove the cover of the bearing near pulleys. Trace the outline of the bearing on the base it is resting on as in operation three. Then loosen the screws holding it down. You can now tilt the shaft and remove the grinding wheel nearest to the screw and the tubing separating it from the other wheel, and after that the other wheel. The flanges (flat discs of metal next to the wheel) will usually adhere to the wheels. Take them off as they will have to be reused. Now put your new wheel or wheels in place, each between flanges. Do not remove the paper discs glued to the wheels by the manufacturer. They serve as cushions. Now reverse the process, being sure that all bolts and set screws are securely fastened in place.

The Water Connection

In cutting we have to have a steady stream of water that can be regulated to keep the work cool and wash away the abraded particles of both the wheel and the stone we are working on. On the B and I, a very small tank is furnished, equipped with a spigot from which the water drips down the horizontally revolving wheels. This means frequent refilling, which is a nuisance. If a transfusion bottle is obtainable from a doctor or nurse friend, this is a great improvement. A hole is drilled in the rim of the machine into which a strong wire is inserted (a piece from a wire clothes hanger) and suitably bent to hold the rubber tubing a few inches above the wheel, so that the water drips onto the wheel just ahead of the spot which is used for cutting. These

The best way to supply water, particularly for the grinding operation, is a circulating pump.

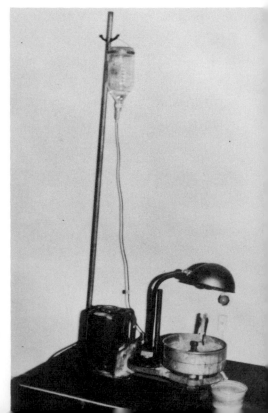

A transfusion bottle is a good source of water supply, particularly for faceting operations.

bottles contain a quart of water and have to be refilled much less often than the cup-size containers that come with the machine. A one pound coffee tin is set under the drainage hole to receive the drainage. This has to be watched, of course, so it is emptied regularly.

On vertically running wheels, water is usually sprayed from above from a water connection built into the splash guard. The water for this can come from a direct connection with the city water supply. If a plumbing job is done connecting the unit rigidly to the general plumbing system, it will create a cleaning problem and will have to be disconnected every time you change wheels. If a hose connection is used, be sure to use high pressure hose. I once used ordinary garden hose and took an involuntary shower. The best system is a recirculating system using a small pump. A very effective one is manufactured by Beacon Engineering. Here, all one has to watch is that the return hose is not clogged. Otherwise the pump will dry up.

I have found it a good idea not to immerse the end of the hose coming from the splash pan of the grinder in the receptacle containing the water that holds the pump, but to suspend it a few inches above this container. This keeps the hose from being air bound and, since the drip is visible, helps further in detecting a possible clogging of the hose.

A feasible inexpensive way of supplying water is to use buckets with spigots soldered on at the bottom line. These buckets should be hung about two feet above the grinding wheels. A sprinkling can may be used to carry water from spigot to buckets. The outflow of the splash cans may be connected to the sewer line directly or caught in buckets, which have to be emptied periodically. In each case be sure to flush the waste line with a strong stream of water after you stop work to keep the grit from plugging up the plumbing.

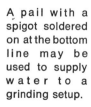

A pail with a spigot soldered on at the bottom line may be used to supply water to a grinding setup.

Sawing

When I first took up lapidary work, the literature on the subject still gave much space to the mud saw, a device in which the cutting was done by a metal blade to which a mud consisting of abrasive was fed. Except for the fact that the blade was revolved by an electric motor, this was similar to the method used for millenniums by cutters in the Orient.

The diamond saw at that time was just coming into vogue, and instructions were still given in the manuals on how to notch the edges of a blade of mild steel, insert the diamond dust into the notches, and peen it in. Today diamond saws are relatively so inexpensive and made so well that it would be silly to make one's own. In these commercial saws the diamond is sintered into the metal in one way or another. They all do fine work as long as used correctly, and there is no deforming of the edge. This can happen if the edge is hit so as to

A common brick is used to sharpen a diamond saw.

chip it, or a stone while being cut is twisted out of the plane in which it is being cut, thus jamming and blunting the blade. Always make sure that the rough to be sawed is held firmly in the vise. Most saws are now available "ready to cut." But occasionally a new blade seems to be "blunt." In that case take a few cuts into an ordinary brick or, better yet, a refractory brick (the kind used as furnace lining). A piece of carborundum wheel can be used. This treatment will also restore saws that "glaze" after cutting a lot of very tough material such as, for example, rhodonite. This treatment will abrade the metal on the edge of the blade, thus exposing the diamond particles which do the actual cutting. Some saws may carry directional arrows indicating in which direction the blade is supposed to run. Always heed this direction. For some blades the manufacturers claim that they can be run in either direction. Once such a blade is run in one direction, keep it running the same way.

There are two kinds of sawing devices: slabbing saws and cutoff saws. Slabbing saws usually swing blades from twelve inches up, have a cover, and are best run in oil. They are made to slab material held rigidly in a vise. They usually come with an automatic feed device and a cross-feed arrangement for the vise, thus permitting a number of slices to be cut from a given block of material. The jaws of the vise are lined with wooden slabs. The rock is clamped between these slabs so that the saw cuts into it as close to a right angle as possible. A little deviation from 90° does not matter with a good rigid blade and automatic feed, but if the angle is·too steep the saw may be squeezed to one side, thus ruining it. It may sometimes be necessary to saw a

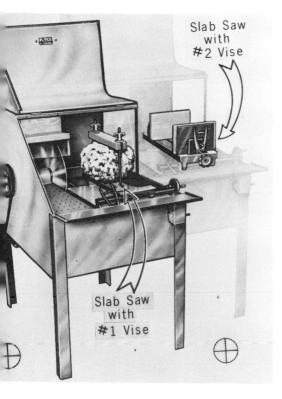

Slab Saw with #2 Vise

Slab Saw with #1 Vise

A slabbing saw. *Photo, Covington Engineering*

The blade of a 16-inch saw.

Make sure that the material is held rigidly in vise when sawing on the slab saw.

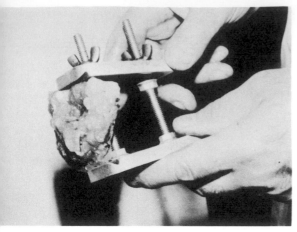

A slab grabber.

A slab grabber is used to hold odd-shaped material and is, in turn, held in the vise of the slab saw.

flat side or even two on a piece of rough to be able to hold it properly in the vise. Odd-shaped pieces, particularly those with sharp edges, may be sawed by fastening them first in a "slab grabber," which, in turn, is held in the vise proper. Adjust the vise so that the stone is a few millimeters from the saw and then engage the lever that makes the automatic feed work. To clean the sludge from the bottom of the saw tank is dirty work. A helpful tool can be made from a square oil can. Cut it off diagonally.

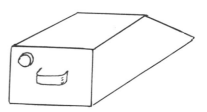

A scoop for cleaning out sludge from the bottom of slabbing saw tank can be made from a square quart can, by cutting it diagonally.

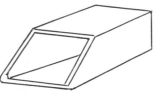

Cut off along this line and bend the resulting raw edge back on itself to stiffen it. Use this to scoop out the sediment and deposit in a bucket. The empty drum in which the cutting oil came is fine for this. Let the sediment stand for some time and pour the clear oil which eventually rises to the top back into the saw sump.

The trim saw is essentially used to cut slabs into blanks. It does not have a hood or automatic feed. If a vise is provided, it is usually a clumsy affair which, as a rule, has to be pushed by hand. It is best

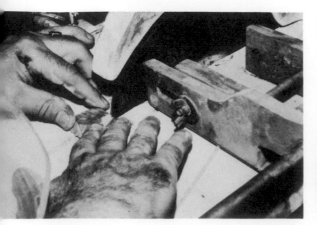

A fine, pink tourmaline from Mesa Grande, California. *Toronto Museum.*

(*below left*) A sodalite snuff bottle, with top of red jasper. Work of the author.

(*below center*) Topaz. *Harvard collection.*

(*below right*) A brooch of various stones cut and set by the author. The stones are, starting at top right, clockwise: moss agate, chalcedony, labradorite, unakite, carnelian, amazonite, red jasper.

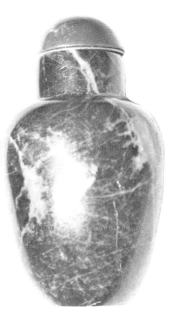

A panoply of gemstone jewelry and carvings, work of the author. *Photo, Michael Walter.*

A faceted synthetic ruby, cut by Dr. Charles Sheer, a pupil of the author.

The author with a fine collection of gemstone rough. The center is a c through a petrified tree trunk owned by Sam Sankman.

The brooch featuring one stone from each state, given by the American Federation of Mineralogical Societies to Mrs. L. B. Johnson.

A pendant of three citrines, cut by the author.

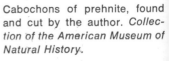

Cabochons of prehnite, found and cut by the author. *Collection of the American Museum of Natural History.*

Gem rough, from top left clockwise: smoky quartz, malachite, rose quartz, lapis lazuli, rose quartz.

A pendant of lapis lazuli on a piece of lapis rough.

Amethyst and synthetic topaz, cut by the author.

A fine slice of agate from Great Notch, New Jersey, polished by the author. *Collection of the American Museum of Natural History.*

Teardrop cabochons of lapis lazuli, Montana agate, and prehnite, cut by the author.

A round and a teardrop cabochon of marcasite in agate from Nopoma, California, cut by Mrs. Fay Pough.

Emerald-cut amethyst, cut by the author.

A brilliant-cut amethyst, cut by the author.

(*below*) One faceted and six cabochon-cut carnelians from Sterling Brook, New Jersey, found and cut by the author. *Collection of the American Museum of Natural History.*

Snuff bottles of gem materials, starting at the top right, clockwise: rhodonite, malachite, unakite, serpentine, malachite. Center: tiger eye. Work of the author.

cooled by water. However, it must be remembered not to let the saw stand in water for any length of time when not in use. If the saw tank has a drainage plug, fasten a hose to it, the other end of which is elevated above the water level in the sump. This makes it easy to drain when not in use.

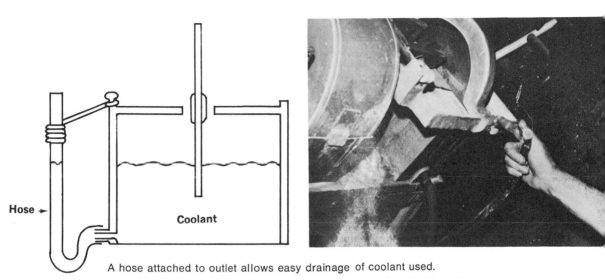

Hose →   Coolant

A hose attached to outlet allows easy drainage of coolant used.

If there is no drainage arrangement, the saw table has to be removed to empty the machine. This is usually fastened by just a couple of screws. A length of small rubber hose is then filled with water, and one end of this, stoppered with a finger, is then immersed in the saw tank. The other is lowered into a bucket below the tank. When the finger is removed all the water will drain into the bucket. In either case the saw blade is then sprayed with oil from a pressure can or wiped with an oily rag to preserve it from rusting.

Pouring water into a trim-saw housing is usually done with the saw in motion. Pour the water in through the slot in which the saw is running until a steady thin spray runs from the saw guard. If you add too much water sop it up with a sponge. It is a good idea to replace the 2 to 3-inch guard strip usually furnished with the saw, which is supposed to catch the spray escaping from the saw guard, with an equally wide thin Plexiglas strip 8 to 10 inches high.

It is essential to present the slab to be cut always so that the saw cuts into it at a right angle. If a diagonal cut has to be made in a slab, first cut a notch at a right angle to its outline, close to the line to be cut. Then only turn the slab so that the saw now cuts into one angle of the notch. The notch should, however, be wide enough so the set of the saw is not ground away by one edge of it. If necessary take two little cuts close together to make the notch wider. It is possible but not

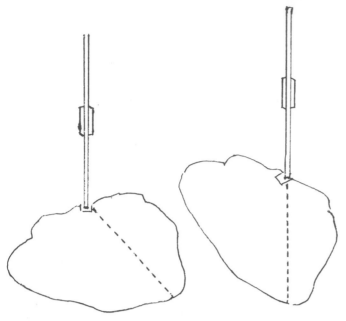

If a sawcut is to be made at a slant to edge of material, first saw a notch at right angles.

recommended to hold a small nodule by hand while sawing it on the cutoff saw. This should only be done if there is one good flat surface that can be rested on the saw table while guiding the rough into the saw.

A trim saw may also be used without the vise to slice small pieces of rough if it has one flat plane to sit on saw table and is held rigidly.

There are small-diameter, very thin diamond saws made to cut valuable rough, usually faceting material. The idea is to save expensive material from being ground away into dust. These are made from phosphor bronze or steel. The bronze ones are preferable for the amateur, since they do not rust away if by accident the sawpit is not drained between times of use. The first time I used one of these, it was a revelation how much faster it cut than a thicker blade. Do not use these thin blades for cutting agate or similar material unless money means nothing to you.

Small saws are specially made to carry extrathin blades to slice valuable rough, such as faceting material or opal.

Should you own a machine on which the saw is mounted on the shaft carrying the rest of the tools, it will usually be found that the saw is held by a reverse thread. To hold the shaft stationary while removing the nut that holds it in place, the only effective way I have found is to use a small pipe wrench. This may mar the shaft a little, but this is unimportant if the wrench is used in a place that no part has to be slid over in taking the machine apart.

Use of the B and I

As pointed out before, a good way to start cautiously in purchasing machinery is to buy one of the small machines that come equipped with a minimum of cutting, sawing, sanding, and polishing discs to enable one to do a reasonable work with a relatively small outlay of money. B and I Manufacturing Company was the first to put such a machine on the market, and in the following, I will refer only to the B and I while talking about this type of machine, both for simplicity's sake and because I am very familiar with a machine of their manufacture.

Like any compromise a compromise in machine guise has some inherent disadvantages as well as advantages.

The advantages of such a machine are its low purchase price and its compactness. The latter makes it portable and possible to store in a small place. The disadvantages are mainly that one has to change wheels for every operation and that cutting on a horizontally running wheel and saw is not as easy as on the same tools running vertically.

There are other drawbacks. One is the water supply. These machines usually come with a small pot to supply water. This is mounted on the rim of the machine and not only is it in the way, but it has to be refilled all the time. This can be fairly easily remedied by using a transfusion bottle as a water source.

The main drawback is that the machines come without instructions. I vividly remember my first acquaintance with it. I had the advantages at that time of having had some lapidary instruction and a friend who helped me set up the machinery. This can be done in two ways. One can either mount the motor shaft at right angles to the machine shaft or mount it parallel.

When mounted parallel the belt does not have to be twisted. It will work more efficiently and have a longer life.

The pulley of the motor is mounted at a 45° angle to the pulley on the B and I.

The pulley of the motor here is parallel to the pulley on the B and I machine.

Cutting on the B and I

Grinding on the B and I should be done on the rim of the wheel for the shaping. The flat top side of the wheel should be used only to obtain flat surfaces. The cutting is, of course, slow compared to vertically running wheels. Wheels soon lose their shape and are hard to dress. It can, however, be done by using a diamond wheel dresser, resting in the notch of the part that is furnished to hold the sawing vise. If a ½-inch shaft is available, on which the grinding wheel can be mounted vertically and which is equipped with a tool rest, the operation can be performed a lot more easily.

All grinding is done on the periphery of the wheel, with the exception of flat grinding, which is done on the flat side of the wheel.

When installing the machine be sure that the small grease cup at the low end of the shaft is filled with cup grease and tightened as far as it will go. From time to time it has to be retightened as the grease is used up, and eventually it will have to be refilled.

The motor should be so installed that the wheel runs toward the cutter in the opposite direction to the way in which the screw rotates that holds down the wheels. Otherwise the screw is constantly loosened.

Sawing on the B and I

In using the saw furnished with the machine, you may have the experience that it works slowly when new. In that case, as mentioned before, put a piece of ordinary brick into the saw vise and cut into it until you find that the saw is "cut in."

To hold the stones to be sawed in the vise furnished with the machine, use small short pieces of wood as cushions, for without these it is impossible to clamp the stone securely. Always try to dislocate the stone by hand before you put it to the saw, for if you succeed, the saw most certainly will, too, and may be ruined in the process.

Fasten the stone so that the saw bites into a surface as much at a right angle to it as possible. Use very little pressure until the saw has

Stones to be clamped for sawing must be cushioned with small strips of wood.

cut a small kerf for itself. Then it is all right to increase pressure, but never push so hard as to slow the saw down. Use lots of water to keep the saw lubricated. Dry it well after use. If there is a chance that it may not be used for a long while, wipe it with an oily rag.

Sanding on the B and I

The B and I comes with a sanding disc fastened to thin felt mounted on a wooden disc. This arrangement is practically useless so far as I am concerned. One can remove the felt and replace it with a rubber disc on top of which sanding cloth can be glued with either rubber cement or some of the other cements recommended for this purpose.

There are a number of alternate ways to sand with the B and I. One of these is the use of rubber-bonded wheels. The grit in these wheels is held together with hard rubber instead of ceramic material as in the grinding wheels. These wheels do a good deal of abrading, and I have used them successfully to rough in facets of large stones.

The best sanding results on the B and I will, however, be achieved by using maple-wood discs on which a mixture of carborundum grit has been painted with a small brush. These are for sale at most suppliers of lapidary machinery but occasionally hardwood discs, which were intended to be used as lamp bases, can be found at hardware surplus stores. If the disc is very smooth, it may be necessary to roughen it with a piece of hacksaw blade to make the grit adhere to the wood. The flat side of the wood is used mostly, but the rim may serve occasionally. It is a good idea to use one side of a wooden lap for cabochons. If it gets a groove worn into it, this may be an advantage. The other side is kept as straight as possible for sanding flats. If it can be obtained at all, a wooden lap with a concave rim is the best of all as it will retain the grits and water, while a flat disc will throw them off and has to be remoistened with the abrasive mixture whenever it shows, by discoloration, that it is drying out. This type of lap, however, has to be custom-made. It is not available commercially.

Polishing on the B and I

Polishing can be done by using a rock-hard felt wheel. If this is of first quality, no support is needed. If not, a thin aluminum or wooden disc may be used to support it. Another possibility is a thin leather disc glued on a hard rubber disc, then glued on a wooden support. For polishing jade, a piece of hard leather held on the top of a wood or iron lap without cushioning is useful.

A hard felt wheel charged with tin oxide is the best polishing arrangement on the B and I.

A wooden lap with concave rim, used with loose grit in water, is a fine piece of equipment, but unfortunately not made commercially.

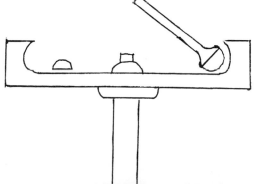

2

Cabochon Cutting

WE ARE NOW MORE OR LESS equipped to go to work. All that is needed is some material to work on.

It is fortunate that the easiest materials to work on are also the least expensive. In general we will be working mostly with the quartz family of mineral. This family has two branches: crystaline quartzes and cryptocrystaline (the crystals of which are visible only under a microscope). Crystaline quartzes in common use are clear quartz (rock crystal), rose quartz, smoky quartz, citrine, and amethyst.

The cryptocrystaline quartzes in turn are subdivided into opaque and translucent or transparent, or a mixture of the two. The opaque if attractive in color is called jasper. If drab in color they are referred to as chert or flint. The translucent to transparent kind is named chalcedony, and the mixtures are agate. Each of these has numerous subspecies. For example, green jasper with some red admixtures is called bloodstone, orange to red chalcedony is called carnelian. Agate has hundreds of subspecies deriving their nomenclature from place of origin, color enclosures, or just pure fancy. Agates occur all over the United States, particularly in the desert regions, and are imported widely from Mexico and Brazil. In the eastern United States they occur as vugs in traprock, but are rarely large enough or attractive enough to cut. On the beaches of Lake Superior they have weathered out of the same material. Gem materials will be discussed in more detail later on.

We will go into the various cutting materials at a later place in more detail.

To begin we obtain a moderately sized slice of jasper or agate about ¾ inch by one inch and about ⅜ inch thick. It should be free of

Templates of various shapes are used to outline the stone wanted on a blank of rough material.

Hold the template firmly on top of the material and draw your outline with an aluminum pencil.

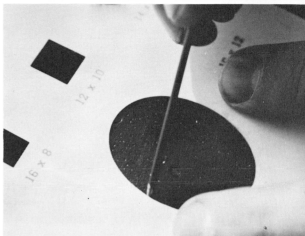

fractures and pinholes and if possible of attractive color and design. We choose an opening on the template that gives us as large a cabochon as the material will allow. It is best to start with an oval shape, because that is the easiest to cut. The template is held firmly in place on the material which has been put down on a solid flat surface. We draw the outline of the chosen oval with an aluminum pencil, keeping the point as close to the lower edge of the opening as possible. It is best to go over the line several times to be sure it is clearly visible. Now the surplus—the part of the rough that is outside the line—has to be removed. If there is very much of it, particularly if some of the overlap is large enough to make another stone and if we are the lucky owner of a trim saw, the surplus can be sawed away. How to do this correctly has been explained earlier.

The tip of the pencil should be pointed toward the edge of the template.

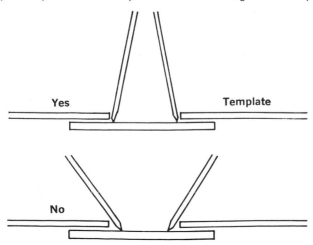

Yes   Template

No

After the blank is marked, all the surplus outside of the aluminum line is ground away.

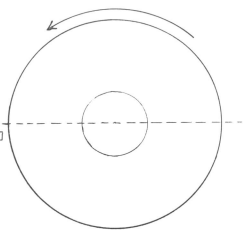

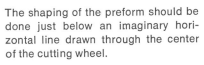

The shaping of the preform should be done just below an imaginary horizontal line drawn through the center of the cutting wheel.

At present let us assume that our blank is small and that the outline chosen covers most of it. In this case we will grind the surplus away. Note that the marked side will be the bottom of the stone. Cutting should be done at the highest speed possible, because the wheels will work faster and are less in danger of being deformed. Under ordinary circumstances, it would be advisable to regulate the transmission belt so that it runs over the largest motor pulley and the smallest pulley on the shaft. However, since this is our first attempt, we will arrange for the slowest speed possible. (Just the opposite of the above.) This permits better control while we get used to our work. Thus a false move will not be quite so disastrous. Now we turn on the water and the motor switch and go to work.

The cutting should be done on a level just below an imaginary horizontal line drawn through the center of the shaft on which the grinding wheels revolve.

The forearms of the operator should rest firmly on the rim of the splash pan. This will help to keep the operator's hands from accidental contact with the grinding wheels, which can abrade the skin and cause nasty cuts.

There should be enough water so that it is thrown off the wheel in a fine spray, but not so much as to drench the operator and surround-

The forearms of the operator should be resting firmly on the splash pan. Note that light source is arranged between operator and work.

The drawing on the left shows how *not* to approach a cutting wheel with a piece of jagged rough. The one in the middle shows the correct way. By turning the stone in the direction of the arrow, the point will be ground away (as seen on the right) without damage to grinding wheel.

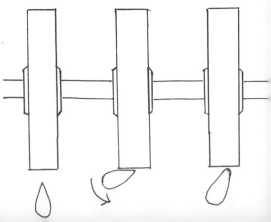

ings. Even so, a rubber apron that covers the cutter from below the neck to ankle is a sound investment. The piece of rough to be worked should be large enough to hold with both hands. Approach the work to the wheel gingerly. If there is a sharp point on the cutting material, round it off gently by beginning to grind on a flat plane adjacent to the point and turning the rough so that the sharp edge is eliminated. This will avoid gouging a hole in the grinding stone that will enlarge with every revolution and result in a bumpy wheel. From the beginning get used to moving the work back and forth over the entire cutting surface of the wheel, remaining about twice as long near each outer edge of the wheel as its center. This will keep the cutting surface as flat as humanly possible. Hold the slice being cut so that the material is cut away at a 90° angle to the marked surface. The idea is to end up with an oval the upper rim of which still bears the marked outline. By checking your progress at frequent intervals, it is possible to accomplish this on your first stone without any difficulty. The next step is to cut a very small bevel on the very edge, partially cutting away the aluminum outline at an angle of 45° to the flat bottom of

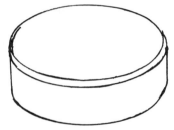

A small bevel is ground around the outside of the bottom plane of the preform, which will partly erase aluminum outline.

the stone. This can be done on a sharp new sanding cloth mounted on a drum sander or on the stone on which the outline was ground. In the former case a fine line of white powder will form along the edge cut. By keeping this line, which is easily visible, to an even thickness the bevel will be uniform. In using the cutting wheel one has to be very careful not to overcut. This bevel should not be more than about one millimeter wide on a stone of 20 × 30 mm. On a larger stone it will, of course, be a little wider, and it will be narrower on a smaller one. The bevel, small as it is, has several purposes. It will make it easier to pick up the stone from a flat smooth surface. It will help the stone to sit flat in a tight setting even though there is a little flow of solder around the inside of the bezel that holds it. A beveled stone will also be less likely to chip when being fitted into a tight setting, and when the top of the stone is formed.

Since it would be difficult to cut the top of the stone while holding it by hand, we now affix it to a short length of doweling about 3½ inches long with a component similar to sealing wax. The length of dowel stick will hereafter be called a dop stick. For stones of small to medium size, a dowel of ¼-inch diameter is just right. For very small stones a tenpenny nail is fine with part or all of the top ground off, if necessary. For larger stones a more substantial stick may be used. There are also rosewood sticks in the shape of old-fashioned penholders on the market. These were originally used for facet cutting with the so-called jamb peg. They are much more expensive but for our purpose they are not as good as the inexpensive dowel because they are too long. Dopping waxes of several kinds and colors are on the market. All are mixtures of shellac with different other ingredients and fillers. Some professionals use clear stick shellac instead of dopping wax. My preference is for a chocolate-colored wax that is marketed in square flat cakes.

To affix a stone to the dop stick the cake of wax is heated over the flame of an alcohol burner, being careful to hold it above and not in the flame so it won't catch fire. (This would consume the shellac component and thus lessen the holding power of the compound.) As the wax softens it starts to glisten. Do not let it get so hot that it starts to drip. When in the glistening stage, start applying the wax to the upper end of the dop stick. Cover the top of the stick and add enough wax to form a blob that comes down about ½ inch on the side of the stick. It should be large enough to form a short cone sufficient to cover the bottom of the stone. It is good to have a tile or small piece of flat stone or glass on hand, such as a discarded pen base, to flatten and shape the dopping compound. Even when hot, the wax will not adhere to a cold surface. It can also be shaped by molding it with the fingers, but, if touched with bare hands when in the glistening stage, it can give a nasty burn unless your fingers are well moistened.

The next step, after the wax on the dop stick is formed to the approximate size of the stone it is to support, is to heat the stone. To do so alternate the stone held in tweezers and the dopping wax above the flame so that both are brought to the right temperature simultaneously. The stone should be uncomfortably hot to the touch but still touchable, and the wax glistening hot. The stone is then affixed to the wax. By putting the stone down on a table and pushing down on the dop stick, close contact is established. Then the stone is reheated on the dop and the wax shaped to support it to the very edge. The stone's lower edge should form a 90° angle to the dop stick in all directions. The stone should be exactly centered on the stick and at no place should the dopping wax hide the outline of the stone. A common

A piece of dowel rod is charged with dopping wax. Then the stone and the wax on the dop are heated simultaneously over the alcohol lamp.

The wax should support the stone to its edge, but should not hide the bevel. The stone's lower edge should be at right angles to dop stick, and it should be exactly centered.

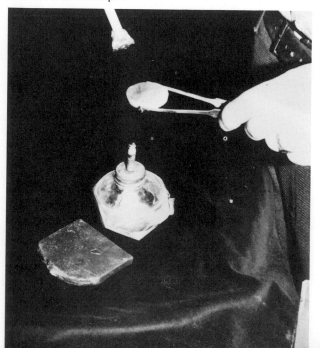

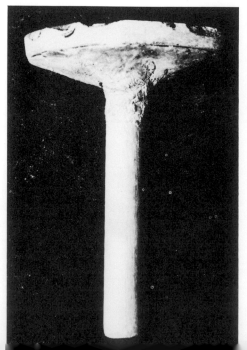

Some mistakes in dopping. From left to right (clockwise): (1) dopping wax hides outline of stone; (2) the stone is off-center; (3) the dopping wax does not support the stone sufficiently; (4) the stone is not mounted at right angles to dop stick.

mistake made by beginners is to waste lots of wax by letting it come down too far on the dop stick. Another is to orient the stone according to the upper edge of the stone. A well-dopped stone is half the battle. Let the stone cool off before beginning to work, since rapid cooling off will cause it to separate from the dopping wax. In the case of a very delicate stone it might even crack.

Next we cut the top of the stone. As a first step we round off its top.

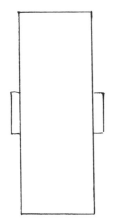

The top of the stone is gradually rounded into a shallow curve. To do this, the dop sticks are held at slight angle to grinding stone.

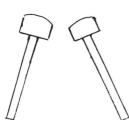

The operation takes place as in cutting the preform, just below the center line of the grinding wheel.

This is done by holding the dop stick at a slight angle to the cutting surface and revolving it, gradually rounding off the stone by stages.

Top View

Side View

Four steps in rounding the top of a cabochon:

The top of the stone has been properly rounded off.

We then cut away the side of the stone beginning at the top, revolving the gemstone against the cutting wheel, until the bottom edge of the stone is reached. This operation is carried out about halfway down the grinding wheel from the imaginary horizontal line.

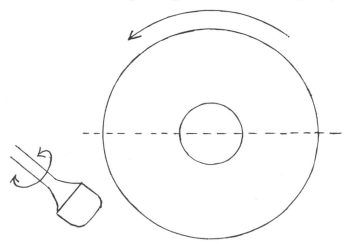

The side of the stone is cut away at a point about halfway down the wheel.

The sides of the stone have been cut away at an angle of 15° to the perpendicular, leaving a slight ridge where they meet the top.

This will leave a slight ridge where the newly cut sides meet the rounded top.

This ridge is then ground away by rapidly moving the stone in a sweeping upward motion. While revolving it rapidly.

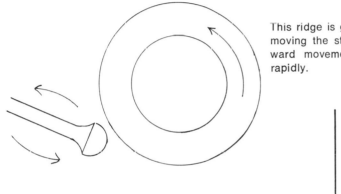

This ridge is ground away by rapidly moving the stone in a sweeping-upward movement, while revolving it rapidly.

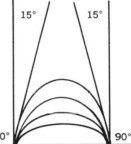

The edge of the stone nearest the base should form a 15° angle to the perpendicular, regardless of the height of the stone.

When this operation is finished, we should have a stone curving evenly in every direction. The edge of the stone nearest the base should form a 15° angle to the perpendicular whether the stone is high domed, medium, or flat. At this stage, while we have a practically perfect shape, its surface will probably show some small flat spots and bumps. If there are two cutting stones of various grit sizes available, we now proceed to the smaller grit size. If, for example, we have been cutting on a 220 grit wheel, we change to 320. (It is advisable to get used to good habits from the start. So shut off the water on the stone you have been using.) If only one cutting wheel is available, the stone can be smoothed off by using very light pressure. In either case, twirl it rapidly to get as even a surface as possible to the very edge. While cutting, check yourself frequently from the beginning. To do so, dry off the stone each time on a paper towel, a piece of rag, or your forearm. The stone must be absolutely dry, as it is impossible to check a wet stone. Feeling the stone with the tip of one's fingers will often disclose irregularities that cannot be seen with the naked eye. To judge your own stone, remember that if you sliced your stone all the slices should be nearly parallel.

Parallel profiles cut through well-made stone at different places should result in parallel curves.

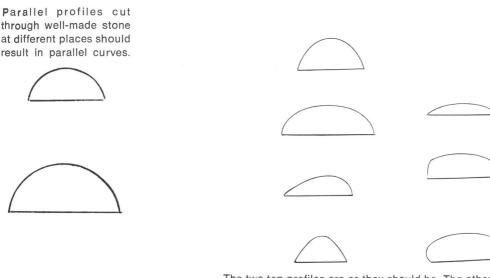

The two top profiles are as they should be. The other five profiles show common beginners' mistakes. In descending order we see an uneven curve, a stone that is cut too steeply, a stone cut with too sharp angles, a clumsy curve, and a stone that overhangs.

Here are some remedies for beginners' problems: if the edge gets too sharp or the stone's outline is lost, take the stone off the dop stick and recut it to a smaller size. If the stone pops off the dop, it was probably not hot enough. It also might have been oily. In that case wash it first with soap and water, then dip it in alcohol and dry before redopping. Some stones are very hard to dop. This can be remedied by giving the stone's back a very thin coating of clear shellac, letting it dry, and then dopping as usual. The clear shellac also comes in handy when, as sometimes happens, the aluminum line washes off too easily. In that case, cover it with shellac, let it dry, and then cut as usual.

Sanding

The next step is sanding. Use of this word is a hangover from the time when sand was actually used for the operation. Actually the same carborundum grits are used from which grinding wheels are manufactured. But they are applied to a flexible surface by being affixed to a cloth called a sanding cloth. This comes in two forms: one can be used dry only, the other can be used both wet and dry. The latter is the right one for our use. It comes in long strips, usually three inches wide, or in discs. The strips are mounted on sanding drums, the discs on slightly convex discs. In either case they are underlaid with a slightly yielding material such as hard felt or rubber. Wetting is done with a moist sponge. The water will help to avoid rapid heat buildups and also will remove some of the debris that accumulates around the cutting. particles, but a stone can be very satisfactorily sanded without moisture. In fact, it is a good idea to start sanding wet and continue until the cloth dries out. The dry cloth will improve the finish. Sanding is supposed to remove the scratches left by the cutting operation. Sanding cloth still has a cutting action particularly noticeable when it is new. Be careful not to stay in any one place or flat spots will appear on the stone. The cutter should experiment with various pressures. It has been my experience that new sanding cloth and high pressure on very hard and dense materials rapidly bring up a partial polish. However, this combination builds up heat fast and it is a good idea to check the stone frequently (every few seconds) for temperature against the palm or forearm. If it gets too hot it will "burn," that is, white spots will form on or just below the surface. It also will transmit the heat to the dopping wax, causing the stone to "fly off the handle." Sanding should leave a smooth near polish on agates. It can be improved by going to smaller grit sanding cloth, particularly if it is somewhat worn. It is advisable to wash the stone and your hands well when going from one operation to the next. Watch for scratches on the very top of the stone, which would indicate a flat spot there. If it does not yield easily to sanding it may be necessary to go back to the fine grinding wheel. Be sure to sand all scratches on the periphery.

It is good to have available a choice of sanding cloths of different grits and different degrees of wear. The invention of expandable sanding drums has contributed greatly to the variations of sanding made possible by the ease of changing sanding belts. To revive the action of worn sanding cloth, temporarily apply a mixture of loose abrasive grit and water, 320 size if much work is to be done, 600 grit if the stone is already fairly smooth. An old sponge, a piece of rag, or even a paper towel, is useful to apply the mixture.

When the stone is smooth all over (examine it with a magnifying glass), wash it well. Use a brush on the stone, dop stick, and your hands so all grit is removed. Then proceed to polishing.

Polishing of agate is done mostly on cushioned leather or on felt

A well-sanded stone should appear nearly polished.

Stones may be polished on padded leather discs.

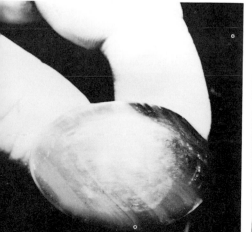

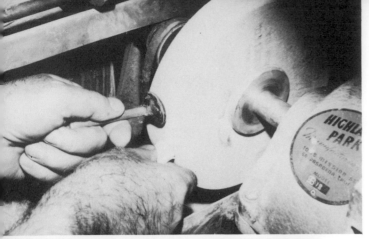

Alternate polishing may be done on hard felt wheels, running either horizontally or vertically.

Polishing powders may be applied with pads made from rolled-up linen strips.

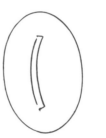 

The acid test of a well-cut stone: if a fluorescent light reflects as smooth curve, all is well; if the reflection is unevenly distorted, the stone should be recut.

using oxides either of tin (tin oxide) or cerium (cerium oxide). As an intermediate step the microscopic silica skeleton of long-extinct minuscule sea animals called tripoli is used. The powders are dissolved in water and painted on the leather or felt with a brush or on small pads made of rolled-up linen strips. The polishing powders go a long way; small amounts are actually better than heavy concentrations. Once the leather or felt is well impregnated, only water has to be used in order to keep heat down. Again the stone is rotated rapidly, first on the tripoli, then on the cerium or tin oxide. Each polishing powder must be used on a separate disc. If the sanding has been well done, it should take only a short time to bring up a first-class polish. A first-class polish should not show any scratches under magnification. The surface should reflect a straight line, such as a fluorescent light strip, bent according to the curve of the stone, of course, but not as a wiggle. Our first stone is finished unless we want to polish the flat reverse of the gem.

An easy way to remove the finished stone from a dop stick is to immerse it for a little while in a bowl with ice water or put it into a refrigerator or freezer for a short time. Since most of us are impatient to hold the finished stone, we can also resort to the more expeditious

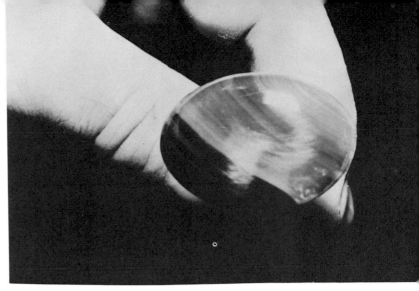

Our first stone is finished.

method of reheating the stone and the wax that holds it in the alcohol flame. When the wax is soft, the stone can be pushed off with the blade of a knife. Any wax still adhering to it may be scraped off with a pocket knife. There is no need to worry about harming any stone with a hardness on the Mohs scale of more than 5 (see Chapter 5), since it is harder than the knife. To remove the last traces of wax, the stone is immersed in a small jar with alcohol, scraped again if necessary, and then wiped dry. It is a mistake to attempt to pry a stone off before the wax has softened sufficiently. Many good stones have been ruined in this manner.

Alternate Methods of Sanding

A stone can also be sanded by using the tub type of machine on a maple or other (hard)wood lap, using loose grit either in water solution or in oil solution.

There are also rubber-bonded wheels for sanding that can be used wet or dry. The manufacturer recommends them particularly for the harder stones such as sapphire, ruby, and chrysoberyl.

The Problem Stones

Having finished one stone you have employed all the operations of cabochon gem cutting. However, there is a lot more to it, because different materials respond differently to treatment and even the same materials occasionally require different methods if the result is to be a perfect stone.

The following is a list of operations and materials that can be varied in your attempts to produce a worthy stone:

Grinding

1. Speed of cutting
2. Kind of grit—carborundum, diamond
3. Size of grit
4. Hardness of bond of cutting wheels
5. Pressure

Sanding

1. Speed
2. Kind of grit
3. Size of grit
4. Material grit is applied with or to:
   Cloth (new or worn)
   Paper
   Rubber
   Loose grit on wood
5. Application wet or dry
6. Cushion under sanding cloth—hard leather, rubber of different hardnesses, felt

Polishing

1. Speed (usually low)
2. Material:
   Cerium oxide
   Tin oxide
   Chromium oxide
   Stannic oxide
   Linde A
   Levigated alumina
   Very low micron carborundum
   Diamond
   Tripoli
3. Form of polishing material:
   Dry powder
   Watery solution (in varying proportions of powder to water or oil)
   Oil mixtures
   Stick form
   Commercial mixtures
4. Carrier of polishing compound:
   Wood
   Leather
   Felt
   Canvas with or without beeswax
   Lead-type metal
   Tin
   Plastic
   Muslin buff
   Cast iron
   Pellon
   Ultralap
5. Pressure
6. Varying degrees of moisture

There are a few problem materials that we will encounter frequently. In the cabochon field these are rhodonite, lapis lazuli, serpentine, and jade. The faceting problem materials are peridot, garnet, tourmaline, and apatite. I know of dozens of other problem gems, but they are rare and the average cutter will never handle them. The cabochon materials mentioned above have this in common: while they do not offer any difficulties in the cutting and even may sand just like the common quartz, the trouble comes in polishing.

Grinding and Polishing a Flat Surface

To obtain a perfectly flat, perfectly polished surface is one of the most difficult operations in gem cutting. The larger the surface, the greater the difficulty. Flat surfaces are, of course, polished extensively in faceting, but I am referring here to flat surfaces on specimens and the bottoms of cabochons. If a cabochon is made from a sawed blank, it has, of course, one or more flat surfaces. If the stone to be ground is to be shaped from a pebble or rough fragment, it has to be studied carefully for its potential. If it is large enough to furnish two or more stones, it can be sawed. If it can be held in a vise for this purpose, so much the better. If too small or oddly shaped to be held in a vise, it may be dopped to a piece of wood and sawed with the wood held in the vise. If it will furnish only one stone, a flat plane will have to be ground. This is done by holding the stone between thumb and forefinger of both hands and moving it against the wheel, always holding it in one plane. The wheel should be very flat. The stone should be moved from side to side of the wheel and up and down, moving in one plane while grinding.

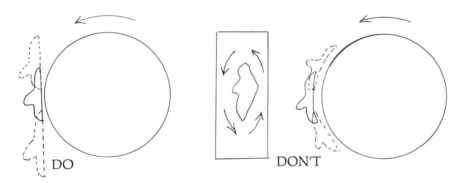

DO   DON'T

A flat surface may be ground by moving a piece of gem material up and down and sideways, always in one plane. The picture on the left shows the correct procedure; the picture on the right shows how it should *not* be done. The picture in the middle shows the frontal view of the operation.

It should not be rocked back and forth in a rotary motion. Once a fairly flat surface has been achieved it can be made truly flat on the side of the wheel. During this operation the stone is held with one hand, while the other holds a moist sponge against the side of the wheel above the stone. It takes an astonishingly long time to reach a perfectly smooth surface, but perseverance always wins.

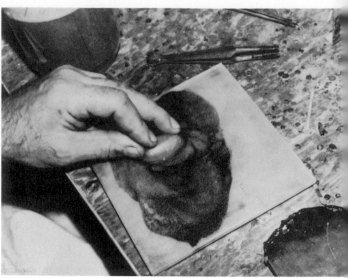

A flat surface can be trued on the side of the grinding wheel. Water must be supplied by a sponge held in one hand.

A flat surface can be achieved by using a mixture of water and carborundum grit on a glass plate. The whole surface of the glass should be used.

Many people are against using the side of the stone but I have never found any disadvantage in this practice.

Another way to create a flat surface is by grinding the stone by hand on a piece of plate glass or plate-glass mirror. A small amount of loose grit is dropped on the glass, moistened with a few drops of water to the consistency of thin cream. The flat is moved back and forth and in circular sweeps covering the whole surface of the glass so as not to deform it. It is good to start with 220 grit until a uniformly flat surface is reached. Then wash stone, hands, and glass, and repeat the operation with 600 grit. Check results frequently by washing off the grit and drying the stone. No one can tell results by looking at a wet stone. The grit breaks down as work progresses, which is all to the good. If the grit stops cutting, it has to be replaced from time to time.

Flats may also be ground on a revolving flat cast-iron lap to which a watery solution of grit is applied.

Once the flat surface has attained maximum size, which means that it will accommodate an outline for the largest stone that can possibly be produced from the given material, we draw the outline for the stone to be cut. To hold it for this purpose, it is a good idea to have a piece of Styrofoam or similar material handy. By pressing the irregular top into the plastic it is easy to hold the template steady on the newly ground flat surface.

It is not advisable to polish the flat side of a cabochon before shaping it to size, since a polished surface is practically impossible to mark.

Sanding can be done on a flat wood lap, scored and painted with silicon carbide in water or oil emulsion. A drum sander may be used if the rules mentioned above for grinding a flat surface on a pebble are followed. Amateurs usually do not polish the bottoms of opaque or near-opaque stones. On translucent stones, particularly of light color, it enhances the beauty of the stone; on transparent ones it is practically a necessity. Polishing is accomplished on a wood or Lucite lap with cerium or tin oxide if flatness is important. If a little rounding off is not objectionable, a felt wheel can be used. By far the best way to polish a flat, however, is on Pellon. Pellon is a plastic material that can be purchased at most lapidary supply stores. It comes as ready-cut discs with adhesive already applied. Pellon is not a polishing agent but just a carrier of the polishing medium. For quartz, a solution of cerium oxide in water in the thickness of light cream is applied. Use just enough to moisten the surface well. Hold the stone on the Pellon, moving it back and forth using moderate pressure. A polish will appear incredibly fast. In using Pellon, watch for the following:

1. Put the Pellon on the supporting disc tightly so that no air blisters are formed below the material.

2. Do not let it get soggy nor let it dry out or get hot.

3. Do not stick any sharp points into the Pellon, thus gouging holes.

Pellon, being a soft material, will slightly round off the edges of a flat polished surface.

For ordinary use this does not matter. If you intend to enter the stone in competition it will just have to be done the hard way. You will then have to face the fact that somehow surfaces which appear to be perfectly flat take a polish around the periphery, leaving a stubborn spot in the middle that refuses to polish. You may prefer to use Pellon and not to enter competition. Let your conscience be your guide.

3

Faceting

FACETING IS AN ATTEMPT to improve on nature. Nature for her own good reasons has created transparent gem materials in many shapes and colors. But it was left to man to take this material and prepare it so as to show its colors to the best advantage, trim it to eliminate flaws and to give added symmetry, and arrange surfaces so that a maximum of light is thrown back at the beholder of the finished gem.

Faceting has been carried on in one form or another for a long time, but the scientific use of refractive indices and correct angles is fairly young. Benvenuto Cellini found it necessary to back diamonds with colored metal foil to improve their reflection. Mechanical faceting heads of various kind, cost, and ingenuity are now on the market and permit even a rank amateur to do good work.

Many professional lapidaries still use a rather primitive system, the jamb peg, which is an inverted wooden cone with evenly spaced indentations all over it. A long dop stick, resembling an old-fashioned penholder, is used to mount the gem on. The angle of the dop stick is adjusted by using higher and lower holes in the jamb peg. It takes considerable practice to produce good results with this method, but once learned it is of course speedier than mechanical devices. An improvement on this method is the Willems facet head. This uses grooves in an aluminum cone and a fishtail dopping device. It is rather difficult to adjust the height of this cone by the fractions called for by the different thickness of cutting and polishing laps. This can be counteracted by using a cutting-polishing sandwich, that is, mounting polishing and cutting discs on the spindle of the lap at all times with a paper disc in between to avoid contamination. When cutting, turn the cutting lap topmost; when polishing, reverse.

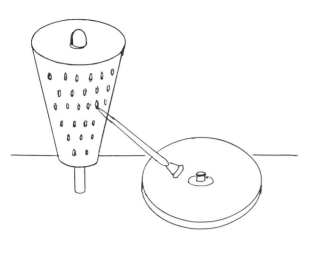

The Willems facet head is an improvement on the jamb peg.

The most widely used faceting devices manufactured for the amateur are more highly mechanized. They consist of discs revolving in a horizontal plane, which do the cutting, a stationary but movable mast at right angles to the plane the discs revolve in, a movable arm that at one end is loosely connected to the mast in such a way that it can be raised or lowered. The other end carries the gem to be cut and polished. The connection to the mast usually carries a pointer and dial to indicate the angle at which the stone rests on the lap. It also has a rotating device numbered so as to give the cutter a way to expose different areas of the gem to the lap to be cut.

It would be very difficult for me to choose the faceting unit I would like to be stranded with on a desert island. They all are finely designed and well-made instruments and their prices are very similar. I consider it a great advantage, however, to work with a unit on which the whole handpiece can be removed for inspection of the stone and replaced in a simple motion. Being a member of the middle class, oppressed by high taxes and kids in college, I also looked for a low-priced unit, which I found by combining a Lee faceting head with a B and I six-inch unit. The complete Lee assembly would of course be an improvement on this setup. I learned faceting on the jamb peg and

A Lee facet head mounted on a B and I is a very economical arrangement.

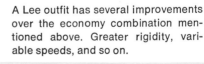
A Lee outfit has several improvements over the economy combination mentioned above. Greater rigidity, variable speeds, and so on.

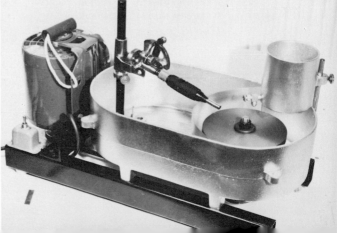

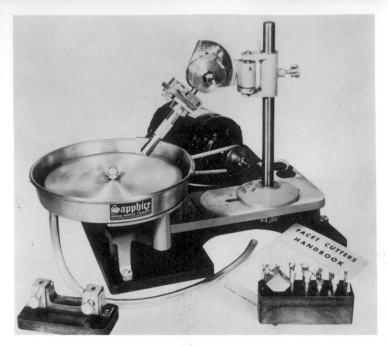

A Sapphire faceting outfit is another example of the many fine faceting setups available. It offers a number of clever gadgets built to fit it and to cut the more complicated stones.

have tried the Willems head. Someday I would like to buy two additional machines, one of them being the Sapphire faceter. It is a good idea for a would-be purchaser to look over a number of different units either at a dealer's who stocks them or at one of the larger shows, where usually some of them can be seen in action.

The Cutting Lap

Until a few years ago facet cutting was done on cast-iron laps on which an emulsion of cutting grit in water was painted. This was messy but satisfactory and cheap. Today, practically all cutting of facets in this country is done on diamond impregnated laps. These may be of copper or brass or bronze into which the diamond dust is pushed by main force. They may be metal discs the surface of which is covered with a thin layer of plastic impregnated with diamond, or the diamond may be sintered into the surface of metal laps. Copper or copper alloy laps may be bought charged or uncharged. The hobbyist can save himself a lot of money by charging his own lap.

Charging a Diamond Lap

To charge a copper, brass, or bronze lap, lay it on a sturdy table covered with several layers of newspaper. You need a small bottle of oil, a carat of diamond of the desired grit (600 and 1200 are the most widely used), and a hacksaw blade or a piece of one. Use the hacksaw to score the lap surface with lines about 2 millimeters apart and crisscrossing in all directions. Brush off the loose particles. Put a few drops of oil on the lap surface. Now deposit small dots of diamond powder the size of a pinhead in two circles about the lap. One of these circles should be about 2 inches from the edge, one about 4 inches in on a six-inch lap. The dots of powder should be about 1¼ inches apart. Gently distribute the powder with a fingertip. Do not rub it in just yet. No powder should be deposited in a circle of about 1½ inches around the arbor hole, but the lap should be covered to the outside edge. Now press the diamond into the metal with either a steel roller

A broken hacksaw blade is a good tool for scoring a lap. Scores should run in all directions.

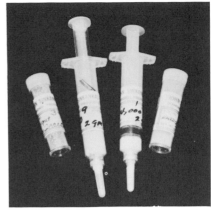

Diamond for charging comes as dry powder in plastic vials or mixed with a carrying agent in small plastic syringes.

The diamond powder is distributed in dots the size of a large pinhead in a pattern all over the lap. The spots of powder in the picture are overlarge for better visibility.

or a wedge of agate or jasper at least an inch wide, the bottom of which has been ground into a slight convex curve. At the beginning of the process the diamond makes a gritty noise which disappears as it is imbedded. With the agate use both a rocking and a rubbing motion and go over the whole surface many times, using as much force as possible. Twenty minutes to half an hour should do the job. Mark the disc clearly with the size of the grit by scratching the numerals into the lap close to the arbor hole. It is possible to charge each side of a lap with a different grit, but I find it advisable to use different laps for different grits. If I charge both sides of a disc, I use the same grit. About ½ carat will properly charge a 6-inch lap. A disc can be recharged when the diamond wears off.

A steel roller is used to push the diamond particles into the metal.

An alternate method is the use of an agate wedge to impregnate the metal with diamond.

Polishing

Polishing of faceted stones is also done on flat laps. These can be made of copper, tin, lead, a mixture of tin and lead with antimony, called type metal, wood, and Lucite. For quartz gems, Lucite is used most.

Polishing powders are metal oxides such as tin oxide and cerium oxide, also finely ground synthetic alumina (Linde A), and very fine diamond powders.

Beginning to Facet

Faceted stones come in all kinds of shapes: round, oval, square, heart-shaped, drop-shaped. On the modern mechanized faceting setup, the easiest to cut is the standard brilliant (a round stone). We shall do one of these as our first lesson in faceting. We choose a suitable piece of either clear white or smoky quartz and cut it into a preform. The preform should look like half an onion on top of a center slice of tomato of equal diameter.

LEVEL OF GIRDLE

A preform should look like half an onion set on top of a slice of tomato.

A blank of clear quartz is shaped into a preform for a brilliant.

The "tomato slice" part should be about ⅓ of the height of the whole stone, the "onion" part ⅔. The whole should be 80 percent as high as wide. It is half the battle to have an exactly shaped preform. The profile can be checked against a homemade template cut from cardboard or thin metal, or else the stone can be mechanically preformed by mounting it on a dop with the table of preform attached to the dop, which is then inserted in the handpiece of a flexible shaft. The stone is shaped by holding it against a piece of grindstone immersed in water in a tin can. Again the roundness of the stone should be carefully checked in a template or by sticking the preform through the hole of a metal washer. It is important to check for roundness at the level where the girdle is going to be on the stone.

After we have shaped our preform, the first facet to be ground is the table. It is ground perfectly flat. A small bevel is then ground all around it. This will eliminate the possibility of small pieces of the

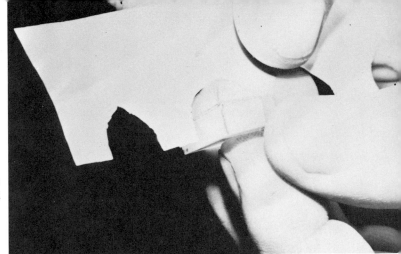

The profile of the preform may be checked against a homemade template.

A preform may be shaped by rotating it on a flexible shaft against a grindstone immersed in water.

To mount the preform for holding it in the handpiece of the flexible shaft, small metal discs are soldered to finishing nails.

The important line to check for roundness is where you plan the girdle to be. Here a washer is used to do so.

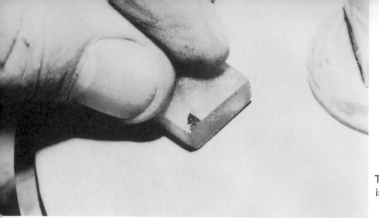

To smooth the table, the stone is best held by hand.

Some people prefer to grind and polish the table while holding it in a 45° adapter.

Lee Manufacturing recently brought out a 90° dop holder for grinding and polishing the table of faceted stones.

edge crumbling off in polishing which might then be dragged over the nearly polished surface causing scratches. (See grinding a flat surface, page 43). It is then held by hand on the revolving 600-grit diamond lap until the surface is entirely free of visible scratches and is velvety smooth.

We now change to a polishing lap. This could be a Lucite disc charged with cerium oxide or it could be any hard flat lap covered with Pellon. The polish will come up much faster with the Pellon lap, using

A set of various dop sticks. One has a square-cut preform mounted on it.

A hollow cone and V-type dop stick.

cerium oxide in water solution. There are, however, purists who claim that Pellon rounds off the edges of a facet and does not leave an optically flat surface. This sometimes is true. But the edge of the table is going to be ground away anyhow and the surface will be distorted only in rare cases, probably when the crystal we are working on is badly twinned. In such cases the thing to do is to regrind the table surface and polish on Lucite. If you take your faceting very seriously and have a lot of time to devote to it, you can, of course, stay away from Pellon altogether.

It is advisable to use as a first stone one which is neither too large nor too small, a stone of 10 to 12 mm is just about right.

Some people prefer to grind and polish the table after dopping. To do this either a 45° dop (made by M.D.R. Manufacturing Co.) or a newly introduced 90° dop holder is used (made by Lee Manufacturing).

Next we dop the gem. On all mechanical devices known to me, the dop stick is a short length of metal, usually brass. One end of this dop usually has some keying device so that it can always be inserted in the handpiece in the same position. The other end is either a round flat disc or is hollowed out to permit seating of the pointed pavilion (the bottom part of a faceted stone) with the cone thus formed.

There are some dop sticks with wedge-formed hollow heads for the accommodation of square and emerald cuts usually called V-dops.

The manufacturer apparently intends the flat-surfaced dops to hold gems when they are dopped table side down. I much prefer to use the hollowed-out dop for this purpose also, since the dopping wax in the recessed cone holds much more securely.

There are two schools of thought in cutting a faceted stone: one starts on the crown, the other with the cutting of the pavilion. I prefer the former method. Thus the next operation is to select a dop stick hollowed out on top just slightly smaller than the diameter of our gem. The dop stick is charged with wax. This calls for heating it well to be sure that the wax will adhere to the metal. A hollow dop stick usually is charged only by filling the inside of the cavity. The stone is heated and pushed point first in the softened wax.

Now a dopping block is called into play. This device is an elaboration of a triangular indentation in a block of wood, or metal, permitting us to line up two dop sticks exactly.

A dopping block.

A stone is dopped and
centered.

Some have an attachment, at right angles, in the very center, in which a pointer can be inserted to help in centering gems. This is very helpful, particularly in the case of square stones. We now select a dop with a flat surface approximately the size of the table on our stone (dop #1) and insert it on one side of the transfer jig. If there is a means of fastening this dop down, do so. Then reheat the dop with the stone attached and insert it in the other side. The table of the stone should touch the flat side of the stoneless dop. Now push the heated dop in the direction of the stone. This is done to seat the stone as deeply as possible in the wax and to line up the table exactly parallel to the surface dop number one, which means that it is at a right angle to the dop sticks. If the preform was exact the stone will be perfectly centered. If not the stone and dop will have to be reheated and the stone pushed by hand until it is dead center, with the table still exactly at right angles to the dop.

Lift the dopping device to eye level and slowly rotate the dopped stone. No light should show in any position between the two surfaces.

The stone at the left is properly seated, centered with the table at right angles to the shank of the dop. The stone at right is off-angle.

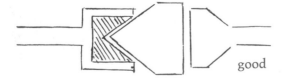

good

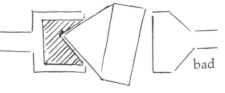

bad

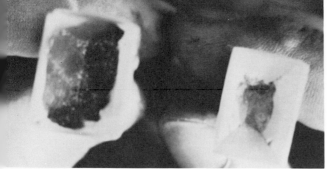

When looking through the table, the dopping wax will be seen adhering to the pavilion if the stone is well dopped. The stone at the right will come off during faceting.

good   bad

The stone at left is not seated properly. On the right, the metal walls of the dop touch the stone as they should.

Looking down into the table the adhering dopping wax should show as a well-centered dark circle or square, as the case may be. If this spot is not uniformly dark, in the light areas the dopping is not adhering properly to the stone. This should be corrected by reheating.

The stone should be seated all the way down in the dop.

Here are some difficulties which may be encountered. The surface of dop #1 must be perfectly clean. If any grit is adhering to or embedded in it, it may scratch the polished table facing it. To make sure it does not, cover the surface with Scotch tape. The wax may not adhere to the dop, particularly if it is new. Slight roughening with a file of the surface to which the wax is supposed to adhere and washing the dop first in soap and water, then in alcohol, will help. The shellac trick which we mentioned to make stubborn stones stick can also be used here.

Most faceting devices are calculated to work with the left hand of the cutter holding the dopping arm.

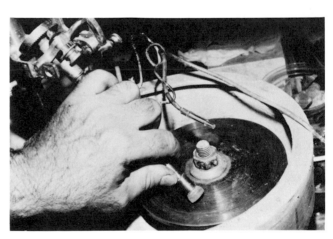

On most faceting setups, the handpiece is held in the left hand.

This leaves the right hand to regulate the water, wipe the gem for inspection, handle the magnifier for inspection, and so on. But if a cutter wants to reverse the procedure there is no law to keep him from doing so.

Our stone, now well dopped, is inserted in the handpiece. We are

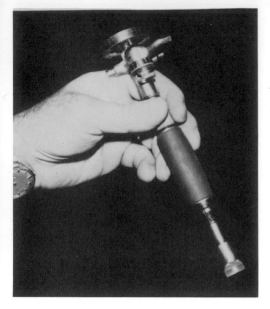

A dop is inserted in the handpiece.

ready to cut a standard brilliant. We mount the (diamond) cutting lap on the spindle of the machine.

A standard brilliant looks as follows:

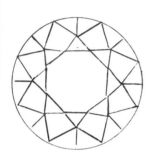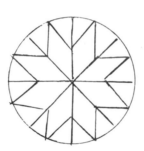

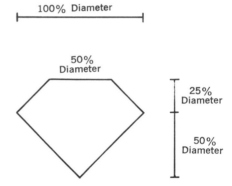

100% Diameter

50% Diameter

25% Diameter

50% Diameter

The diagram on left shows the arrangements of facets for the crown for a standard brilliant. The diagram on right shows the facets of the pavilion of this cut.

Most brilliants are cut to the approximate dimensions on this diagram.

Do not panic at this seemingly complicated array of lines. Also remember that, unless you are cutting for the market or competition, slight digressions from the norm are not fatal.

Faceting devices and cutting instructions come with all kinds of different indices on their dial. The conversion chart shown here makes it possible to reconcile differences.

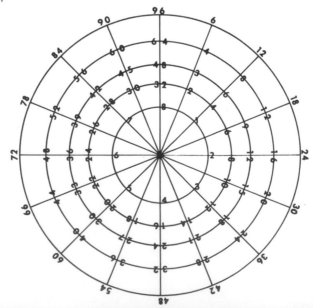

Assuming that we start with a 64 index dial, adjust the head of the handpiece so that the indicator located there is engaged in the notch next to that number. Then adjust the dopping arm at an angle of 42°. This means that the pointer of the faceting device is set at 42. Turn on the water to a slow drip, set the lap in motion, and gently lower the stone to be cut onto the lap. Look at the stone within a few seconds. A diamond lap's cutting action is deceptively gentle. Particularly with a new lap, material is removed very rapidly. So get used to checking progress continuously. The smaller the stone and the facet, the more essential is frequent inspection.

When the first cut is down to about ¼ of the height of the stone,

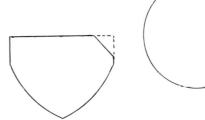

A side view (left) and top view of the first cut on a brilliant.

The main facets of the crown are cut in.

turn the stone 180° and cut your second facet at 32 to the same depth, then turning the stone 90° cut a third at 16 and finally a fourth at 48. If your preform was exactly round and all facets are cut at exactly the same depth, you should now have a perfectly square table. We now cut the edges off the square to obtain an octagon at dial settings 8, 14, 40, 56. If against all expectations you have a perfect octagon, you now enlarge the facets all around until the table is just a little more than 50 percent of the width of the stone and the facets are cut to about ⅓ of its depth. If you are not experienced, there is bound to be some deviation from a perfect cut. This is why I advised cutting the facets somewhat shallower at the beginning than they will eventually have to be cut. If the facets of the stone meet in a perfect octagon at the table, but some facets are larger than others, your preform was not perfectly round. You either take the dop out of the handpiece and correct the fault on a grindstone or sharp sanding belt (600 grit), or, if the deviation is slight, correct it on a sanding belt with dop stick in handpiece. If one facet is larger than the others and is cut lower on the girdle than the others, all facets must be enlarged slightly until they join the girdle at the same level.

If one facet of the stone is smaller than the others and does not quite come down to the same level as the two adjacent ones (these will be a

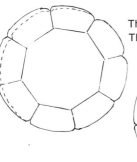

This stone is out of balance because it is not perfectly round. The dotted line indicates the necessary correction.

This stone has one facet that needs to be enlarged to bring it into balance with the others.

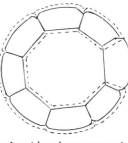

On this stone, one facet has been overcut, all the other facets have to be enlarged.

little larger than they should be), the facet that is too small has to be enlarged. This will cut down the two adjacent facets. Eventually your stone will be in balance. You then raise the adjustment on the masthead and cut the table facets at 30° at 4, 11, 20, 28, 36. The table facets should meet in the center of the line formed by the meeting of table and main facets and go to about the middle of the mains.

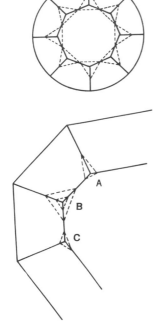

The top diagram shows all the table facets cut in correctly (dotted lines). The bottom diagram at C, shows a trial facet cut at too high an angle and at B, a trial facet at the correct angle.

The table facets have been cut in and blackened with marking pencil for clarity.

To be sure that this will happen, just barely touch down on the stone, then look at it. If the miniature facet thus cut promises to have the right shape when enlarged continue to cut it to the correct size. If the facet is too narrow at the top change to a slightly lower angle and vice versa.

Make a note of the new angle in writing, so that you will remember the exact setting when it comes to polishing.

Cut these facets in rotation; check often since they are so small. Do not overcut. It is easy to enlarge a facet which is too small, but to make it smaller means recutting all adjacent facets. When all crown facets have been cut, the girdle facets are added. These are cut at approximately 45° at dial settings 2, 6, 10, 14, 18, 22, 26, 30, 34, 38, 42, 46, 50, 54, 58, 62. These facets should meet in the center of the mains and just touch the point of the table facet. A trial cut should be made here also to be sure of the correct angle.

This leaves the main as a kite shape. Should by chance any of these facets be overcut, it means going back to recutting the mains. Unless a bad mistake has been made, this is not difficult, just tedious. All these maneuverings probably have brought down the girdle line to about ⅓ the depth of the stone where it should be. We now proceed to polish.

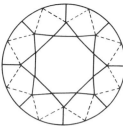

The girdle facets have been cut and blackened.

The top figure shows the girdle facet cut in. The bottom figure at A shows a trial facet at too high an angle; at C, too low an angle, and at B, at the correct angle.

Polishing

Polishing of quartz is best done on a Lucite lap with cerium oxide as polishing medium. In the bad old days we polished with a water suspension of the polishing powder. This called for luck and judgment. If the proportion of polishing powder was too high, scratching developed, brought on apparently by "balling" of the cerium oxide. If too low, it did not polish. The solution had to be added constantly. All this has been changed since my friend and colleague Walter Stone hit on the bright idea of mixing the polishing powder with oil. Any oil will actually do, but boiled linseed oil will eventually dry up thus bonding the powder residue to the lap. For best results, score the Lucite with a hacksaw blade, crossing the scoring so that the surface looks as though it were covered with a fine net. Make an emulsion of a small amount of polishing powder in oil to the thickness of heavy cream. Anoint the scored lap lightly with the mixture, put the lap on the spindle, break it in by rubbing with a flat piece of agate and you are ready to polish. However, you must use a light drip of water or the process will not work. As the polishing mixture works into the Lucite the lap will be usable for a long time without adding any new polishing mixture.

In polishing, the main facets are usually polished first since they are larger than the other facets. It is, therefore, easier to make adjustments if in changing from cutting to polishing you are not "dead on."

Lucite laps are used to polish facets of quartz gems.

Set the angle at 42, the dial at any of the main facet settings, drip a little water on the oiled disc and apply the facet to the lap with considerable pressure. If all is well a polish will show up within a few seconds. Be prepared, however, that all may not be well. Usually there are slight differences in the slant of the cutting and polishing laps.

If only the top of a facet shows a polish, the cutting angle must be raised.

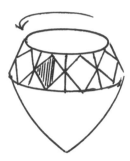

If only one side of a facet shows a polish, the stone must be turned by the cheating device in the direction of the side on which the polish appears.

If the facet is polished near the table but the bottom near the girdle shows scratches, raise the angle slightly. If the scratches are at the top, lower the angle; if one side of the facet is smooth and the other cloudy, turn the gem in the direction of the cloudiness.

The up and down adjustment of angles is done by lowering or raising the point at which the dopping arm is attached to the masthead. It is a bit confusing at first that, when this attachment is lowered, the angle at which the gem is cut will be raised, and vice versa. The small sideways corrections are made by the cheater arrangement (*see* glossary), which is incorporated in all faceting heads. It permits sidewise corrections of the way the gemstone touches the cutting or polishing lap to position between the notches in the index dial. The small up and down movements are made by the screw or micrometer adjustments provided on the masthead attachments. It is a good idea to inform yourself how the cheating device on your machine works before you do any extensive cutting. Should your first facet, by luck, come out perfectly, use the cheater on the second, just to see how the turning of the stone is accomplished.

It is important to realize that polishing can deform a facet to such an extent that recutting on the diamond lap may be necessary. Never, therefore, try to avoid adjustments by pushing just a little harder.

Shown here is the cheating device of the Lee facet head. It is set at 56 in this picture. By loosening the knurled button, the black disc with the five incised lines, just above it, can be turned to right or left. This permits slight sidewise adjustment of the stone to be cut.

This applies particularly in the situation in which beginners sometimes find themselves—namely that no polish appears at all on the facet they believe they are working on. This then calls for a careful inspection of the stone. It will usually show that there is a little bright spot on one of the corners of the facet. If this spot is on the tip of the facet near the table, the angle setting is much too low and must be raised. If it appears at the bottom of the stone near the girdle, the angle setting must be lowered. If it is either at the left- or right-hand corner of the facet, a mistake was probably made in setting the index. If both inclination and angle are badly off-line, one of the rims of the facet will show a polish either wholly or in part. This calls for a correction of both elements. The correction by cheater should be made first, and the angle corrected afterward.

Once a good polish is achieved on one of the main facets, the rest of the facets usually will offer little difficulty. If, however, you get confused because a number of adjustments have been made on one facet and it is still not correct, it is a good idea to go on to the next one, and come back to the first when the correct solution has been discovered.

When all facets are perfectly polished, you remove the dop from the handpiece. Then the most difficult operation—transferring—begins. You choose a dop slightly smaller in diameter than the polished surface. With a rag or towel moistened in alcohol you wipe the polished stone to remove any traces of oil. You put the dop with the partly cut stone into the transfer jig and fasten it down. Now charge the new dop with wax. For this purpose the metal dop has to be well heated. While the wax is still soft press the new dop straight against the stone so that all surplus wax is pressed out and an imprint of the polished surfaces appears on the wax of the new dop.

Now reheat the dop, insert it in the same position in the transfer jig and, while firmly pressing the new dop against the stone, heat it over the alcohol flame. This naturally means lifting up the transfer device.

Heat the dop from all sides possible. As the dop is heated, it will heat the wax with which it is charged and the wax will heat the stone. It may be necessary to protect the thumb holding down the dop with a thumbstall or piece of cloth. After a while play some of the heat on the exposed part of the stone but not on the old dop and the wax connecting it to the gem. When you think a connection has been

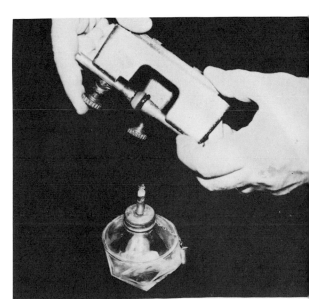

The dopped stone is clamped in the transfer block. A new dop charged with wax is pressed against the polished surface and heated until it adheres to the stone, which then is attached to two dops.

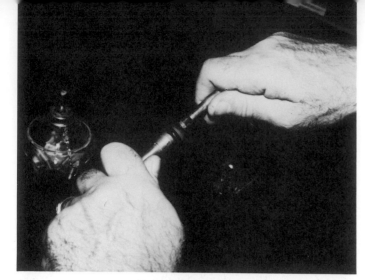

When cool, the assembly is tested to see that the new dop is firmly attached. Moderate pressure is applied.

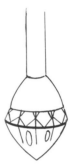

The newly dopped stone is inserted in the handpiece and by trial and error lined up so that the main facets of the pavilion will be in line with those of the crown. Aluminum lines are used as guides.

The first dop is heated until it can be detached. Surplus wax still adhering to the stone is then removed.

established, let everything cool off and lift the gem, now hopefully attached to two dop sticks, out of the jig. Test the connection by twisting firmly but gently. If it comes apart, repeat from scratch. It is better that it come apart at this stage than later when you are working on the pavilion, the bottom part of the faceted stone. If the connection holds, heat the old dop until it can be twisted off without effort and scrape the dopping wax off with a knife.

Next mark the pavilion with lines leading from the lines formed by the intersection of the girdle facets toward the point of the pavilion of the preform. The main facets of the pavilion should be exactly between these lines. Set the index at any of the numbers used for the crown mains and reinsert the dop into the handpiece loosely. Take a trial cut to see how well you estimated. If its edges are equidistant from the lines on either side, you have done well. If the trial cut is just a bit off center, tighten the chuck holding the dop and adjust with the cheater to center it. If it is close to either line, loosen the chuck and adjust by hand. The idea behind this operation is to line up the mains of the pavilion exactly with those on the crown. This does not in any way contribute to the brilliance of a stone, but is something which has been done that way ever since Louis de Berquem, considered to be the inventor of faceting of gemstones.

Adjust the angle to 43° and cut the main facets. They differ from the crown mains in that they meet in a point. Again, do not cut down to the eventual girdle line right away but leave yourself a margin for jockeying a bit. Most people have much less trouble getting the pavilion mains right, probably because their meeting at a point helps the judgement. When all mains are even, there should be a space left— the girdle. On a stone 10 mm high the girdle should be ½ mm, but it

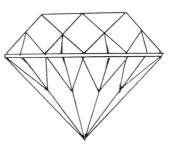

The line separating the crown facets from the pavilion facets is called the girdle. It should not be too large, but if allowed to come to too thin an edge it may splinter when the stone is set.

is better to have the girdle a little larger than to have the crown and pavilion meet in a knife edge. We now add girdle facets. These again should meet in the center of the mains and should go to a point halfway down the main. If the mains are cut at 43° this means the girdle facets will be approximately 48°. Again make a trial cut before committing yourself too deeply. Polishing is done in the same manner as for the crown. If all is well your stone is finished. Some people gild the lily by polishing the girdle. This is done by taking the dop from the handpiece and polishing the girdle on a leather disc such as is used for cabochon work.

Sometimes when everything is nearly finished—usually upon polishing the last main facet—the point of the gem flakes off. This happens probably because the point is touched to the flange holding down the lap or just because of gremlin interference. It is exasperating, but no reason to despair. If your main facets have been cut at 8, 16, 14, 32, 40, 48, 56, 64, cut eight little facets at 4, 12, 20, 28, 36, 44, 52, 60 at a very low angle, 25° or so. These will form a small star which is going to be visible through the table. Because this star detracts from the brilliance of the stone make it as small as possible, just enough to do away with the chipped spot.

Should a small chip flake off the girdle, it is sometimes possible to cut it away by enlarging the girdle a little on a sanding drum and recutting the pavilion.

Some purists are going to be horrified at this suggestion, but I have always held that a beginner should finish a stone even though a little faulty, rather than insist on complete perfection from the very start. This is practical as long as he or she knows what is wrong and will try to do better next time. Nothing will discourage the novice as much as being forced to work away on the same piece of material for too long a time. Nothing, on the other hand, will encourage one as much as to hold one's first faceted stone gleaming in the palm, even though one or another facet is a little crooked.

There is a school of thought that prefers to start the faceting of a stone with the pavilion. In this method the table of the preform is left unfinished until after the transfer. It is then inserted into an angle dop to cut and polish the table, after which the crown is cut and polished. To me the main advantage of cutting and polishing the table first is that it will reveal any flaws in the stone which may have been overlooked. It is also easier to polish a table with the stone held by hand than when held in the angle dop.

Faceting an Emerald Cut

Having successfully cut a brilliant we are looking for new worlds to conquer. The next logical step is to cut a square cut or an emerald cut. Both these cuts are step cuts. This means that the facets on each side of the gem are parallel to each other. The emerald cut differs from the square cut in that its corners are cut off at an angle of 45° to the main facets, thus forming a modified octagon.

The preform for this cut looks like an old-fashioned barn. It is very important to have an exactly rectangular stone to start with. The millimeter gauge is a great help in this operation.

The preform for a rectangular cut looks like an old-fashioned barn.

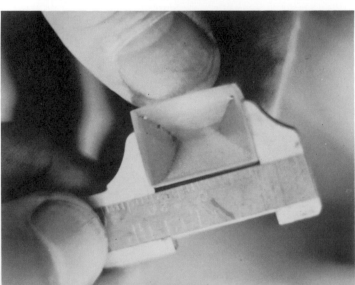

To check the right angles on this preform, use a millimeter gauge.

Again it is important to have the right angle at the exact spot where the girdle of the gem is going to be. Again the table is ground and polished while being held by hand. The stone is dopped table up as for a brilliant. Special V-dops (with a V-shaped notch) are advisable but in a pinch the same dops as used for brilliants may be used with the help of added dopping wax. A three way dopping device, which makes it possible to check that the stone is accurately centered, is a

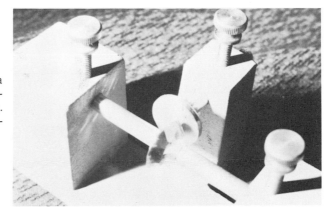

A three-way dopping block is a great help in centering rectangular stones while dopping. Shown here is an Exacto three-way dopping block.

greater help in dopping a rectangular, or later an oval stone, than a round one. Naturally it is just as important to have the table at a right angle to the dop stick as in cutting the brilliant.

Having dopped the stone correctly, we stick the dop into the handpiece loosely without tightening the locking device.

The index should be set so that one of the longer main facets will be cut at the highest number. Theoretically it might, of course, be cut at any setting, but in the beginning it will be a good method and easy to remember. If you are following a diagram, put your stone into the handpiece so that it is lined up according to it.

We now put down the longer side of the rectangle on a lap, with the angle indicator at about 45°. Holding the stone exactly flat we lock the dop into position. Traditionally emerald cuts are proportioned in a ratio of approximately 2 X 3. If the handpiece and dop are equipped with a keying device, ignore it for the purpose of this cut. It is used only for round stones. Now lower the elevating device until the angle pointer is at 90°, or as close to it as possible, and cut a facet. If the preform is 100 percent accurate, the facet will extend evenly

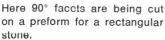

Here 90° facets are being cut on a preform for a rectangular stone.

from side to side of the preform, forming a perfect rectangle. If, as is likely, it is cutting more on one side than the other, adjust by using the cheating device. Cut until this reaches a little more than ⅓ from the edge of the table toward the pavilion. Turn the stone 180° and repeat, then turn 90°, and again 180° from there. We now have 4 facets at exactly right angles to each other.

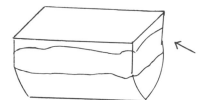

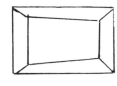

The 90° facets should meet all around the stone, where the girdle is going to be.

It is not important that these facets reach the upper edge of preform as long as they meet in a belt about ⅓ down.

Most of these facets will be cut away in the following operations except a very small strip that will form the girdle. The crown of a small stone will have only two rows of facets. On a quartz stone the main angles would be 40°–42°, the table facets 28°–30°. On a larger stone three rows of facets may be used. These may either be of equal width or the two lower may be equal to each other and the table facet a little smaller. The main facets are cut first. When three rows of facets are used, the one next to the girdle is the main facet, 40°–42°, the table facet is 28°–30°, and the middle facet somewhere in between.

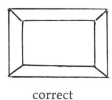

correct   table not square to dop

The picture on the left shows the arrangement of the first four facets on a rectangular stone. The stone on the right was correctly preformed but dopped at a slant.

If the stone is correctly dopped with the table exactly at right angles and exactly centered, the resulting facets will be trapeze shaped with the top and bottom edges exactly parallel to each other. The bottom edges of the facets will meet at the corners and all is well. However, in the beginning, trouble is bound to occur. If the facets are all awry, it is best to check the adjustment of the stone and start all over. If only small divergences occur, they may be corrected by "cheating." However, if just one facet is obtained by cheating it is important to go back to the original setting for polishing on the other facets and also for cutting the next series of facets. If a simple rectangular stone is desired, we can now proceed to polishing.

If an emerald cut is wanted, the corners of the stone are ground off, using the setting between those used for the sides, thus if the sides were cut on 64, 48, 32, 16, the corners are cut at 56, 40, 24, 8.

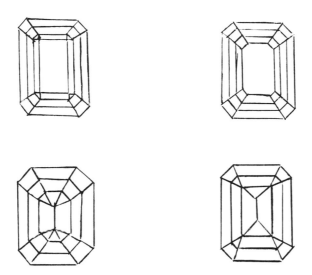

Two versions of emerald cut — above crowns, below pavilions. For clarity's sake, the facets on the crown are drawn too large. The table should be somewhat larger (at least 50 percent of narrow width).

We then transfer the stone and cut the pavilion. This is usually cut with three rows of facets unless the stone is very large, in which case additional tiers can be added. The bottom facet is the main facet.

When cutting an oblong stone, theoretically it is necessary to adjust for height in the same row of facets for obviously otherwise the facets on the long side of the stone will be different from the facets on the short sides. This applies particularly when cutting a large stone and is to be considered seriously if maximum brilliance is desired. Since this doubles the number of adjustments to be made, many cutters ignore the variance and just continue cutting around the stone as though it were symmetrical.

Faceting the Standard Oval Cut

As the third stone to be cut, I recommend the standard oval. Not to be misunderstood, let me say that it will be advisable for the beginner to cut a few brilliants, then a few step cuts and a few emerald cuts to gain skill and confidence with these rather uncomplicated cuts, before proceeding to the oval. The oval is more difficult as it calls for different angle settings for each series of facets. When I did my first oval I followed the instruction in Volume Two of the excellent *Book of Gem Cuts* issued by M. D. R. Manufacturing Company. These two ring books list practically all the well-known facet cuts. These instructions give angles, indices, and order of cutting and polishing, and should be in the library of anyone who intends to do any amount of faceting. M. D. R. also manufactures a very fine faceting machine.

But even so I did encounter a number of difficulties, so I shall give a detailed description of the procedure as I worked it, basing index and angles on their recommendations.

First make a perfectly oval preform; about 15 mm × 25 mm would be a good size. This preform should be straight sided for a little more than ⅓ of its height, with the remaining ⅔ tapering to a well-centered, very blunt point, in character very similar to the "tomato slice plus onion" arrangement recommended for the brilliant.

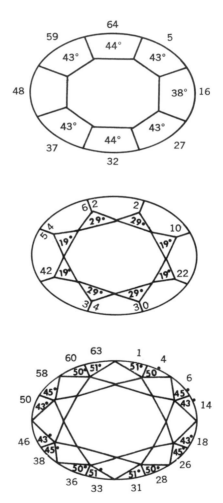

For complicated cuts it is advisable to make a diagram of each series of facets showing both the index setting and the angle to be cut. The three diagrams here show the three stages of cutting the crown of an oval stone.

Then make three large diagrams for the crown, the first one showing the mains with the index in color, the angle below in pencil. The second shows the mains and table facets with the index and the angle figures for the table facets only. The third diagram shows the girdle facets added, this time again the correct figures only for the girdle facets being entered.

Then two diagrams are made for the pavilion which has only two rows of facets.

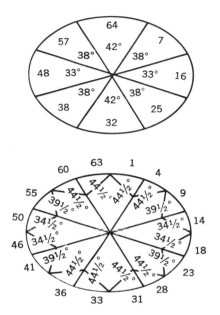

The two rows of facets on the pavilion of an oval stone (the angles worked out are for a 25 mm X 16 mm stone).

Next drop the preform in a V-dop exactly centered and insert the dop in the handpiece so that the stone is oriented exactly as in your diagrams. Now take some trial cuts to make sure that the stone sits correctly in the handpiece. If it does not, readjust the position of the dop in the handpiece. Do not use the cheating arrangement for this. At this stage of the game the preform should be exactly centered.

Trial Cuts

Not Good

Correct

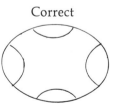

It is imperative to orient the preform for the oval just right in the handpiece. The left diagram shows trial cuts of a badly oriented stone. The diagram at right shows correct orientation (the angles worked out are for a 25 mm X 16 mm stone).

Draw a line with the aluminum pencil on the preform where you think the girdle should be then start cutting your mains. These should come down to near the line you drew, but some room should be left in case, due to some subsequent mistake, recutting should become necessary. In the first attempt, this necessity is a fair bet. The important thing here is to remember that the angles on the diagram are subject to change because of variation of the proportion of your oval preform. If you find it necessary to change this angle, note it on your diagram. The only angles which should be constant are the center mains on the long side and the four mains adjacent to this in order to get as much brilliance as possible. As a matter of course we will find that an oval will not have as great a reflection of light as a brilliant since two mains are cut, of necessity, at much too flat an angle. The main beauty of an oval will, therefore, have to be the beauty of the material.

When the mains are all cut to the same depth, their top lines should delineate the table in the form of an elongated octagon. Corresponding facets should be of the same size.

The next facets to be cut are the table facets. These should come down to about 1/3 of the main and meet in approximately the middle of the mains. They are, however, not symmetrical triangles. Small trial cuts should be made, and the cutting angle adjusted as necessary. While the two sets of four facets are theoretically at the same angle, take nothing for granted.

The girdle facets are cut last to meet the points of the table facets and to touch each other. At the center and end mains, they meet in the middle of this facet, but on the other four the meeting point is not exactly centered.

After all the facets are cut and polished, the stone is transferred and again centered by trial and error. Mains and girdles are cut in the same manner. However, attention should be given to keep the mains at index setting 64 and 32 and the adjoining four main facets at 41° to get as much brilliance as possible under the circumstances.

Difficulties Encountered in Polishing

Sometimes a facet seems to be polishing well but suddenly on inspection two or three deep scratches are discovered. This may be due to a number of causes. It may be that the scratches were there all the time but were obscured by a myriad smaller scratches, which have been polished away. They may have been caused by one or more outsize diamond particles or other contamination in the cutting lap. If continued polishing eliminates them quickly, the conditions that caused them are nothing to worry about. If they get smaller, but persist, the diagnosis that the cutting lap is the culprit is confirmed, particularly if the next facet polished shows a similar condition. The only remedy would be to recut on an uncontaminated lap or else remove the suspected contamination.

This can sometimes be done by dragging a pocket hone over the lap revolving on the spindle while flushing it well with water. This procedure removes metal from the surface of the lap, but not the diamond, and leaves it cutting better. It also very often dislodges pieces of carborundum grit which may have become imbedded. The best stone for this purpose is the so-called Ouachita stone or Arkansas stone (novaculite) but carborundum hones will work. If this procedure still does not remove the trouble, it may be necessary to drag a

If an impregnated diamond lap ceases to cut well, drag a pocketknife hone across its surface. Flush copiously with water during this operation.

well-polished agate over the lap while it is standing still, first from the center out, and then at right angles to locate the exact place of the imbedded impurity. It will then be possible to remove it with a sharply pointed instrument. If this is not feasible, a machinist may be able to resurface the lap.

(If one cannot find a machinist to recut the whole surface, it may be possible to charge it with rough diamond grit for use when lots of material has to be removed fast. John Sinkankas, in an article in the *Lapidary Journal*, recommends etching contaminated laps with sulfuric acid, but I would be scared to do it.)

There may be, however, nothing wrong with the cutting lap. This can be ascertained by inspecting the facets with a strong loupe before polishing. If they are seen to be uniform but show scratches after polishing, the polishing lap is at fault.

Take it off the spindle and scrub it well. Renew the polishing mixture you are using. Scrub the stone and dop as well as your hands. Then try the next facet. If it works, go back to the first facet and try to polish the scratches out. If they are too deep, however, it will be best to recut. Since only a very small cut has to be taken you may get away with recutting only one row of facets. If the scratching still persists, grit may be imbedded in the plastic. In most cases it will be possible to remove it by dragging a knife or a furniture scraper on the revolving lap, thus taking off a thin layer of surface, hopefully including the impurity. If this does not solve the problem, it may be necessary to abandon the lap or at least one side of it.

Some Tricks of the Trade

Beginners often will find themselves with a preform that has a lot of material to be removed. In this case, it is advisable to use as a lap one of the carborundum grinding stones that come with the tub-type machines, cutting until the preform is close to the finished size desired.

In cutting down a brilliant preform that has a lot of material to be removed, it is wise to keep on going around instead of cutting down one facet to the final level, as one will be working on smaller surfaces all the time.

4

Gem Materials

THE MATERIALS AVAILABLE FOR cabochon cutting and faceting are so numerous that in order to keep things uncomplicated, I have in the following list, enumerated only those which in the ordinary course of things we will encounter on a dealer's shelves. I have omitted those which are exceedingly rare or exceedingly expensive. Many are used for both cabochon cutting and faceting and most will yield good results with careful treatment. I am therefore going into detail only where problems exist either in cutting or polishing. To avoid repetition it will be taken for granted that clear and flawless or nearly flawless materials are usually faceted and that flawed, translucent, and opaque materials are used for cabochons.

Materials are listed in alphabetical order, regardless of the fact that amethyst is just another crystaline quartz or that bloodstone is really jasper which happens to be green.

ALMANDINE: Hardness 6½–7½. *See* Garnet.

AMAZONITE: Hardness 6–6½. *See* Feldspar.

AMBER: Hardness 2–2½. Amber is so soft that even with great care it will grind away too fast on ordinary cutting wheels. It can best be worked with hand tools. Preforming and slicing is best done with a jeweler's saw. Shaping can be done with fine files and sandpaper. Worn, very fine sandpaper (600 or more) is used for sanding. Polishing is easily accomplished with tin oxide on a piece of soft leather held in the hollow of the hand. Faceting can be done by using the regular setup as for quartz, but use the laps in a stationary position, moving the gem by hand back and forth. Amber softens at 380° Fahrenheit and melts at 518°–707° Fahrenheit. Never leave it soaking in alcohol, or it will eventually dissolve.

AMETHYST: Hardness 7. *See* Quartz. Amethyst very often is color banded, that is, color alternates in layers. The stone should be cut so that the color bands it presents are parallel to the table in a faceted stone or to the base of a cabochon.

Amethyst comes in a wide variety of shades. The lightest, which resembles rose quartz, is sold under the name Rose of France. If not too lacking in color, it makes a pretty stone. The darker the color, the higher the price. A dark rough with a reddish cast in the purple is called Siberian amethyst, regardless of its provenance, and is the most expensive. Amethyst is sometimes heat treated. This will turn some Brazilian amethyst green. Some amethyst turns to an orange sherry color. This is called madeira citrine and is very beautiful.

APATITE: Hardness 5. This golden yellow facet material is available from Cerro Mercado in Mexico in small crystals at reasonable prices. They cut very easily and fast, but polishing is very difficult. Sinkankas recommends Linde A on a wax lap, but for me this did not work. For polishing, 14,000 diamond on lead or on a new Plexiglas lap that has not been used to polish other gem material seems to be the answer. Chrome oxide Ultralap discs are another solution.

AQUAMARINE: Hardness 7½-8. *See* Beryl. Bluish green to sky blue beryl is called aquamarine. Some light-colored material with more green than blue is within the price range of the amateur. Naturally sky blue stones are very rare and expensive.

AVENTURINE: Hardness 7. *See* Quartz. Aventurine is quartz colored by myriads of small mica inclusions. The color is usually green. This is very difficult to polish since the little particles of mica have a tendency to tear out. The answer is a near-perfect sanding job with fairly new sanding cloth, requiring a minimum of polishing time on leather with tin oxide.

BERYL: Hardness 7½-8. Aquamarine (greenish blue to sky blue); emerald green (colored by chrome); golden beryl (yellow to gold color); goshenite (water clear); morganite (apricot to dark pink).

BLOODSTONE: Hardness 7. *See* Quartz. A dark green jasper with red spots.

CARNELIAN: Hardness 7. Light to dark red chalcedony. Much carnelian that shows a perfect color in the uncut rough will be found to show good color only for a few millimeters below the surface. Stones should be cut with as much of this "rind" as possible. A great amount of the rough from Brazil and most commercially cut stones have been heat treated.

CHRYSOBERYL: Hardness 8½. A small amount of yellow facet material has been on the market lately. Because refraction is higher than quartz, the pavilion angle should be 40°. Cut on 1200 diamond or finer. Polish on tin with 14000 diamond.

CHALCEDONY: Hardness 7. *See* Quartz. Highly translucent to transparent cryptocrystaline quartz.

CHRYSOPRASE: Hardness 7. *See* Quartz. Chrome green translucent cryptocrystaline quartz. Very fine material at medium high prices has been available from Australia. It only pays to get the very best since the second and third grade is not uniform in color and contains small blisters.

CHRYSOCOLLA: Hardness 2–4. Chrysocolla is a soft ore of copper. The material sold under this name is often chalcedony with inclusions of chrysocolla or chalcedony stained throughout by chrysocolla. The former is an abomination and is impossible to polish; the latter is one of the most beautiful materials to work with but fairly expensive.

CITRINE: Hardness 7. *See* Quartz. Lemon yellow quartz, much of it is heat-treated smoky quartz or amethyst.

CORUNDUM: Hardness 9. By my own definition corundum should not be included in this list, since a rough is expensive if it is any good. Corundum comes in all colors from yellow to nearly black; blue corundum is called sapphire—red corundum is ruby. Cornflower blue clear is the most expensive sapphire next to ruby, which is the most desired in a clear blood red color. Much sapphire has inclusions of rutile called silk and, when cut at 90° to the C axis of the crystal, will show a 6-rayed star. The most desired color is highly translucent bluish gray. The only corundum within reach of the average pocketbook is the black star sapphire from Australia. Sapphire can be cut on regular grinding wheels but must be polished with diamond on wood or, better yet, diamond on copper.

EMERALD: Hardness 7½–8. *See* Beryl. Green beryl colored by chromium. This also is really too expensive to be included here. Emerald, even with a lot of feathers, is still considered faceting material.

EPIDOTE: Hardness 7–7½. Epidote is mainly the pistachio green component of the granite known as unakite.

FELDSPAR: Hardness 6–6½.

The Feldspars

There are several important members of the feldspar family available to the cabochon cutter. Many of these are found in abundance and are therefore inexpensive. They are of reasonable hardness, of beautiful color, and take a fine polish.

Common feldspar comes in brownish pink to brown and, while it is not unattractive, is rarely cut in gemstones, probably because it is too easy to obtain.

Blue sodalite is the feldspar most often encountered in the lapidary shop of the amateur. It offers few difficulties. The material, however, often shows what appear to be cracks. It should, therefore, not be sliced too thin. Before starting to cut, it is a good idea to test the material by trying to break it along the cracks, which are apparent, by twisting it, using some force. If it does not part under this treatment it is reasonable to assume that it will hold together in cutting. Irregular, very small lines are acceptable in the final product. This also applies to labradorite, which is a grayish, unassuming-looking feldspar. It shows a gorgeous schiller, mostly blue, but also peacock or golden or a mixture of all these colors if viewed from a certain direction. To find this schiller, the rough has to be wetted. It should be viewed from above, with a light source just above the beholder's head. It should then be sawed in such a manner that the colors show on top of the slice. It is sometimes a good idea to grind a little flat on top of the rough to make sure of the exact plane in which the best color shows: there is no guarantee, though, that a given piece of rough will show the same color in every slice or even on opposite sides of the same slice. It is recommended that you view each slice, and, if necessary, adjust the tilt in the saw vise of the piece of rough being worked. A very small degree of tilt makes the difference between a perfect stone and a mediocre one. It is best to cut labradorite as very flat cabs. There is some transparent labradorite available. This is usually facet cut.

AMAZONITE is a light green to bluish green feldspar. It always shows a lozenge-shaped pattern and sometimes a silvery schiller which adds attractiveness to the finished stone.

SUNSTONE: Resembles common feldspar. It is of a light orange or brownish color but if viewed from a certain direction shows a reflection of many very small gold-colored glittering points. This material should not be confused with a material of the same name that is just glass containing copper filings and goes by the name of goldstone.

MOONSTONE: Moonstone has a pronounced cleavage and should be cut on well-dressed wheels. They are cut in very high cabochons. Moisten the rough and turn under a light just above your head, holding the rough close to your body until a layer of silvery sheen is seen. The stone may be at a slant to the horizontal when this takes place, or the sheen may appear when the stone is exactly horizontal. In the latter case slice the material at right angles. In the former case it has to be sliced at an angle.

FLINT: Hardness 7. Drab-colored cryptocrystaline quartz.

GARNET: Hardness 6½–7½. There are a number of different related minerals going by this name, to wit:

> Almandine
> Andradite
> Essonite
> Grossular
> Pyrope
> Rhodolite
> Spessartite
> Uvarovite

Of these, only almandine and pyrope are commonly available. Recently some rhodolite has come from Tanzania. Cabochon cutting should be done on well-dressed wheels. Polishing on leather with Linde A or 6400 diamond. Polishing of faceted stones used to be difficult, but since the arrival of diamond compounds has become less of a problem. Polishing with 14000 diamond on Lucite works fine.

GOLDEN BERYL: Hardness 7½–8. *See* Beryl.

GOSHENITE: Hardness 7½–8. *See* Beryl.

GROSSULAR: Hardness 6½–7½. *See* Garnet. An occasional small crystal is available from Eden Mills, Vermont, or Asbestos, Canada, from Tanzania, or Madagascar.

JADE: Hardness 6½–7. Two materials are lumped under this name, nephrite and jadeite. While unrelated chemically they work very similarly. Jade comes in all colors of the rainbow from white to purple to gray to green. A chrome green translucent jade is the most desired (Imperial jade). Grayish green to leaf green are most commonly available. Both materials have in common great toughness and an irregular arrangement of the crystal structure. This causes difficulties in polishing. A good sanding job is of course a must. This, at times, is attained on a sequence of sanding cloths, of different grits and degrees of wear. Sometimes a sharp sanding cloth #600 will produce a semipolish. More often it has to be followed by sanding on worn cloth—results vary greatly with pressure—quite often high pressure is successful but occasionally low pressure will do the trick. Jade can stand a lot of heat and heat seems to promote a good polish. To polish jade, most often a mixture of chrome oxide and Linde A on hard leather is indicated. The owner of the House of Jade in Cambria, California, gets a perfect polish by using a rather thick slurry of tin oxide on canvas. I have obtained mirror polish occasionally on tin oxide and leather. 1200 diamond grit on sole leather works when nothing else will.

LABRADORITE: Hardness 6–6½. *See* Feldspar.

LAPIS LAZULI: Hardness 5–5½. Comes from two main sources, Chile and Afghanistan. The Chilean material has usually a heavy admixture of gray matrix; the Persian material is practically all blue. The bluer the rough, the better it will finish. As a rule, a good polish can be obtained by using a mixture of Linde A and chromium oxide in water on hard sole leather, with best results when the leather starts to dry up and pulls on the stone. An 8000 grit diamond compound on wood is an ultimate, if fairly expensive solution.

MALACHITE: Hardness 3½. Malachite is one of the few soft stones that takes a high polish without trouble. The rough usually comes in lumps that show botryoidal development on one plane of the specimen. If sawed parallel to this plane, the most pleasing patterns will develop. If sawed at right angles the material will show only stripes. Great care should be taken to do all operations as wet as possible, since malachite dust should not be inhaled.

MOONSTONE: Hardness 6–6½. *See* Feldspar.

NEPHRITE: Hardness 6–6½. *See* Jade.

OBSIDIAN: Hardness 5½. Obsidian is volcanic glass. It is extremely brittle and should be cut on well-dressed wheels. There are a number of varieties of obsidian from transparent, like a very dark smoky quartz, to coal black opaque. A variety of opaque black with white inclusions is called snowflake obsidian. A mixture of brown and black is called mahogany obsidian. A somewhat translucent kind with silvery bubble inclusion is called silversheen, a version with similar yellowish inclusion goes by the name of goldsheen.

OPAL: Is hard silica gel. The glorious colors we see in some of it are just products of the refraction of light in the internal structure of the stone. There is, however, a lot of opal that shows no such color play. In Australia it is called potch. It is found all over the world as incrustations, usually very thin, and is then referred to as hyalite. Some very colorful red and orange opal without color play, found mostly in Mexico, is misleadingly called fire opal. Opaque opal in green and yellow with dendritic inclusions has recently come on the market. Opal is found in commercial quantities in Mexico, Nevada, Honduras, and Australia. The Mexican material displaying color play furnishes mostly small stones and is often cut to include the matrix (the sandstone in which it is found). The Nevada material has for the most part a very high water content and is as a rule useless as cutting material because it crazes on drying out. Honduras material is not widely available. This leaves Australia as the main source of cutting material for the amateur. A fine Australian opal, shimmering throughout in the colors of Joseph's coat, is one of the most beautiful stones imaginable. However, few cutters will ever have the chance to handle one since the rough is much too high priced. This applies particularly to the so-called black opal, a material with blue black background showing strong flashes of red and green fire. However, there is less expensive opal showing some color play that is still usable. It comes as nearly clear material called jelly opal, as a white milky-colored rough with color bands of greater or lesser width running through it, and as a vein material running through dark sandstone or quartzite. This latter is cut with the matrix the same as the Mexican material. If the bands of color are visible on all sides of the piece of material, cut the stone by grinding away the covering layer of colorless material exposing the color in its full width. In fact, if anything is to be done with a rough having only a thin layer of fire showing, this is the only way to proceed. However, in this case one has to be prepared to find that the color of the side of the seam will be different from the showing at the crosscut and in practically all cases less brilliant. If the seam is wide enough, professionals will slice the rough at right angles to the seam and make it into a number of small brilliant stones rather than a larger stone of indifferent appearance. If, in the case of most amateurs, the only rough you can afford is thin seamed, be very careful not to grind away the paper-thin layer of fire. On the other hand, it may be necessary to grind away all overlay as a very thin layer of potch can hide what little fire there is. If the rough you have has fire but is transparent or semitransparent, it can be made into a doublet by glueing it to some dark material or glueing it to light backing with black opaque epoxy. The trick is to have a perfectly flat back on the opal and a perfectly flat top on the backing material. Black obsidian is often used for this purpose. The stone is finished after the epoxy has set hard. Opal is treated just like any other quartz stone except that it should be guarded from shock, such as bumpy grinding wheels, and from excessive heat in dopping, sanding, and polishing. It should be ground on the finest-grit wheel available. Only the thinnest saws should be used. Because of the high price of the finest of this material, it is cut so as to get the largest stone possible, disregarding standard sizes.

PERIDOT: Hardness 6½–7. Comes in olive green to bright green, the latter color being the most desirable. Getting a polish on peridot was a real job until the availability of the fine diamond compounds. Using 14000 diamond on Plexiglas or Lucite makes it easy. A rough larger than 3 to 4 carats is practically unobtainable. Even in these sizes it is hard to find absolutely clean material.

PETRIFIED WOOD: There are two kinds of petrified wood—silicified wood and opalized wood. Due to the fact that the formation of both was gradual, some of the material will show varying hardness and will undercut. Most petrified wood shows many cracks due to weathering.

PREHNITE: Hardness 6–6½. A lot of prehnite was found recently during the building of Highway 80 through Paterson, and some has been available from New Jersey dealers. It is yellowish to grape green in color and when uniform in texture—which is rare—makes a beautiful gem.

PYROPE: Hardness 6½–7½. *See* Garnet.

QUARTZ: Hardness 7. Quartz is the material most commonly used by the lapidary. It comes in two generically different varieties, the crystaline and the cryptocrystaline. The crystals in the latter are so small that they are visible only under the microscope; they are so compactly structured that a very tough stone results.

The crystaline quartzes:

> Amethyst
> Aventurine
> Citrine
> Crystal
> Rose quartz
> Rutilated quartz
> Smoky quartz (cairngorm)
> Tigereye (quartz replacing asbestos)

The cryptocrystaline quartzes are roughly subdivided into overlapping classes:

Chalcedony: Transparent to translucent unicolored material.

Jasper: Opaque material of good color or design.

Agate: A mixture of jasper and chalcedony showing an attractive design.

Flint or *Chert:* Opaque material of drab colors.

Bloodstone (dark green jasper with red spots)

Carnelian (reddish chalcedony or agate)

Chrysoprase (a chalcedony dyed green by chrome)

Onyx (agate with straight bands)

Petrified wood

Sard (brownish barely translucent chalcedony)

There are hundreds of fancy local and descriptive names for agates, such as Montezuma, Montana, fortification agate, which would fill a small book, all by themselves.

The only agates requiring special lapidary treatment are fire agate which is iridescent goethite encased in chalcedony. It is cut to expose the goethite with just a thin layer of chalcedony to protect it.

The other is iris agate found at certain localities. It will show a rainbow effect if cut in very thin slices and polished on both sides.

RHODOCHROSITE: Hardness 3½–4. Like many of the "soft" gem materials it is hard to polish. But sometimes prolonged polishing on leather with tin oxide will produce good results.

RHODONITE: Hardness 5–6. An ore of manganese, it very rarely can be perfectly polished. It shows an orange-peel effect, which is hard to overcome. The redder the material, the better the chance for a good polish. The deep-colored material is apparently more silicified (and more translucent also). A good sanding job that will hold the polishing time required to a minimum is the answer.

ROCK CRYSTAL: Hardness 7. *See* Quartz.

ROSE QUARTZ: Hardness 7. *See* Quartz. Rose quartz very rarely comes clear enough to facet. There is generally a light veil in the material. This often is an indication of inclusions that may result in star stones if cut correctly. Since rose quartz practically never shows crystal faces, the star can be found only through experimentation. The most commonly used method is to grind the rough into an approximate ball, coat it with oil, and then observe it under a single light bulb to find the points where the stars center. There are two on each globe exactly opposite to each other. Mark these and then saw the globe in half. A star stone should be as high a cabochon as possible. The star can be enhanced by glueing a thin section of mirror to the bottom of the stone. A blue mirror will make a rose quartz stone look like star sapphire to the uninitiated.

RUBY: Hardness 5–9. *See* Corundum.

RUTILATED QUARTZ: Hardness, *see* Quartz. Rutilated quartz is clear quartz shot through with straight hair-thin needles of golden rutile. If these needles are very thinly distributed, the stone can be facet cut. If they are denser but attractively arranged, the stone should be cut in cabochon. It is a good idea to cut free forms featuring the best design of needles possible.

SAPPHIRE: Hardness 9. *See* Corundum.

SERPENTINE: Hardness 2½–3. As serpentine is very soft, it should be ground on the finest stone available with very low pressure and frequent checking. Serpentines are often difficult to dop because for some reason wax does not adhere well to it. Sanding will remove material at a rate much faster than with the quartzes or feldspars. My best polish was attained by using a water solution of 600 carborundum on Pellon applied to cardboard. Do not get Pellon too wet as it will soak through to the cardboard.

SMOKY QUARTZ: Hardness 7. *See* Quartz.

SODALITE: Hardness 6–6½. *See* Feldspar. A blue sodium aluminum silicate, often comes in large masses.

SPESSARTITE: Hardness 6½–7½. *See* Garnet.

SPINEL: Hardness 8. Sometimes found in gem gravel assortments from Ceylon.

SPODUMENE: Hardness 7. It cleaves in two directions, is very sensitive to shock. A good material to stay away from until well experienced.

SUNSTONE: Hardness 6–6½. *See* Feldspar. The best material comes from Norway but there is very fine but dark sunstone from Dover, New Jersey.

TIGEREYE: Hardness 7. Came into being by silica replacing asbestos fibers. The result is a material showing stripes of chatoyance which seem to move as the material is turned. The more thorough the replacement, the better the quality of the cutting material. It comes most often in yellow or yellowish brown, but also in blue or a mixture of these colors. Some tigereye is red as a result of the yellow material having been heated. Tigereye should be sawed in a plane parallel to the original fiber to get the best chatoyance.

The most attractive stones are obtained if the stones are cut with the long axis in the direction of the chatoyant bands. These bands, if viewed at a right angle, appear to alternate light and dark. If a high stone is cut so the division of the alternate colors is exactly centered, an eye-pattern stone will result which is very attractive. Sanding and polishing of tigereye should always be done at right angles to the original fiber structure. A fairly sharp sanding cloth will often give a good finish and thus cut short the time required in polishing. Tigereye is a good stone to experiment with, as various kinds of rough respond differently to treatment. Vary pressure, grits, and so on. All tigereye is sensitive to heat and will spall off on the slightest provocation.

TOPAZ: Hardness 8. Is available in a variety of colors, mostly blue, water clear, and sherry color; the latter is called Imperial topaz and is very expensive. If the rough is of suitable size, it can be distinguished from other gem rough by its relative weight. Because it has a very distinct cleavage, the rough also usually has some flat planes on it which look as though they had some sort of polish. In preforming a topaz rough care must be taken not to have any facets, particularly large facets, in the same plane as the natural crystal facets. Avoid the shock of rough wheels or too sudden rise in temperature while dopping.

TOURMALINE: Hardness 7–7½. Comes mostly in elongated triangular crystals in all colors of the rainbow. Some crystals show different colors along their length, others are red or lilac colored at the core and green on the outside. The most commonly encountered are blue and green. In buying rough do not be seduced by the beautiful color seen by holding it up to the light. If it shows no color unless held up to the light, it is too dark to give pleasing stones. Tourmaline is the classic dichroic material. This means it shows different colors when viewed from two different directions. The blue and green show best colors through the sides of the crystals. Lilac-colored crystals are sometimes equally pleasing either way. Crystals that show dirty pink through the sides often are a good peach color viewed through the ends. A fine polish will be obtained on Lucite with 14000 diamond. Pavilion angles should be 40°.

TURQUOISE: Hardness 6. Comes in colors from greenish blue to sky blue. Uniformly colored dark sky blue gems are considered so valuable as to be used with diamonds in jewelry. It should never be sawed in oil as it will absorb oil and grease and thus lose its color. Weathered turquoise is sometimes impregnated with plastic to harden it and to improve color. Reliable dealers will indicate if this is done. Turquoise with veins of limonite is called spiderweb turquoise and makes very attractive gemstones. Turquoise may be cut on sandpaper and polished on leather with tin oxide without machinery.

UNAKITE: Hardness 6–7. A granite, the components of which are primarily red feldspar, green epidote, and white to grayish quartz. It is hard to polish well because of the slight difference in hardness of its components. A good sanding job with a minimum of polishing time is the answer. A good polish can be had with 1 micron alumina on felt.

VARISCITE: Hardness 4–5. A bluish green gemstone resembling turquoise, but differing from it chemically. Pure variscite handles beautifully and polishes easily, but usually it is cut in a matrix with other phosphate minerals of different hardness, thus presenting the usual difficulties of such mixtures. If the design is pleasing and most of the gem polished, some undercutting is acceptable in this material.

ZIRCON: Hardness 7½. Rarely stocked by dealers to the amateur trade.

Buying Rough Material

There is a great temptation for all cutters to buy too much and too often. Very few of us who have been indulging in the hobby for any length of time have not accumulated more gem materials than we will ever use. There are, however, a few rules in buying rough. If you are interested in purchasing any specific material the best thing to do is go to a local dealer and look at the merchandise he has available. The next best thing is to look over the ads in the magazines and compare the offerings. They will be very similar in price, but occasionally a dealer may have made a special purchase. Never expect to purchase flawless emerald for a dollar a carat. Stay away from "semi-facet" material. It is too expensive for cabochon work and too flawed to facet. There are from time to time large finds made of certain material. A short while ago, for example, there was a glut of fine rhodonite, a little while later a lot of good chrysoprase became available. At such times, many dealers will advertise the same merchandise and prices will be very reasonable. This is a good time to stock up. Don't expect that such a glut will last for a long time. A good way to buy is to go to mineral shows where you can go from booth to booth and compare values. Even though the dealers are all under the same roof, there is often a wide variance in the values offered. It is a good idea to look and listen at such shows. Talk to fellow hobbyists who often are a wonderful source of information on what to look for and what to avoid.

Bargains are not very often the best way to invest your money. I am a great believer in cutting things I have found myself and I have wasted a lot of precious cutting time that way. Once you have gained experience, it is good practice to use the best material you can afford. As a rule of thumb it may be assumed that material doubles in value after being well cut, so it stands to reason that time is spent to greater advantage in cutting hundred-dollar-a-carat emerald than ten-cent quartz, provided one can afford it. One fundamental thought in buying cutting material is that during the last twenty years prices have increased steadily and sometimes, such as in the case of opal, spectacularly.

This, incidentally, is the answer to the question so often asked, whether a professional lapidary can make a living in the U.S.A. The answer is Yes, if he has good enough connections to buy high-priced rough consistently and has a market for his cut stones.

5

Some Theory

WHILE A THOROUGH KNOWLEDGE of crystallography and optics is a great help, it has no place in a manual of beginner's instructions. The following simple facts are good to know, however, and easy to remember.

In orienting rough for cutting, it is sometimes necessary to know how the crystal is oriented. For our purposes, we just have to know the C axis. The C axis is the main axis and is the direction in which the crystal grew when it was formed. Fortunately for us, we can usually recognize it because it is the long axis of a crystal, or else it is at right angle more or less to the plane at which a crystal is or was attached to the matrix. In double-terminated crystals it connects the end terminations. If the material does not show crystal faces, it will be necessary to determine the C axis by means of instruments, which is beyond the aims of this book, or by experimentation. This latter process has been explained at the appropriate place.

The C axis is also important in orienting star sapphires. The star is always at a 90° angle to the C axis.

It has been stated that a faceted gem of clear quartz cut with the table at right angles to the C axis will show more brilliance than one cut with the table parallel to it. While there is no scientific proof of this, it would explain why some quartz gems show more brilliance than others cut with identical angles.

Play of Color, Opalescence, Schiller

A number of gemstones owe their beauty to optical effects. They show colors that are only the result of refraction of light. The opal is one of these.

Many of the feldspar gems show an effect, if viewed from a certain direction, that makes it appear as though there were a hidden light source within the gem, gleaming in one or several colors, pinpoints or stripes of light. To show these effects the rough must be correctly oriented. To do so, moisten the material, then view it under a light source until the color shows on the surface of the specimen. Then cut a small flat, adjusting until the best effect is obtained. Slice the material parallel to this plane. Sunstone, aventurine, labradorite, all members of this family, show the best effect when cut as very flat cabochons. Moonstone, another relation, shows the moon effect best when cut as very high cabochons. Beryl sometimes contains numerous needlelike cavities. If these are arranged in parallel order, a moon will show in a cabochon.

Eye Stones, Star Stones, Chatoyancy

While the light effects in opal and feldspar and beryl are the results of crystaline arrangements of chemically homogenous materials, some moon and star effects are the result of microscopic inclusions of other materials such as rutile. Examples of these are rose quartz, beryl, garnets, and sapphires. Tigereye is still another manifestation of chatoyancy. Here, however, the original inclusions (asbestos fibers) have been replaced by silica which retained the structure of the material it replaced.

To find the star in a stone, the light source should be an incandescent bulb—a clear bulb is better than a frosted one. Fluorescent lights are no good for the purpose.

Refraction

Different gem materials have different indices of refraction. These may be used to identify many cut gems by use of an instrument called a refractometer.

For purposes of the cutter, it is good to have an idea of refractive indices, as they influence the ability of gemstones to reflect light. The higher the refractive index, the lower should be the angles of the main facets in order to get as much reflection as possible. Since there are relatively few materials we use for faceting, we have only a small number of refractive indices to keep in mind.

Apatite	1.633
Beryl	1.582
Corundum	1.765
Garnets	1.745–1.810
Quartz	1.547
Topaz	1.622
Tourmalines	1.610–1.645

In practice this means that the main facets of the pavilion on all quartz stones, feldspars, and beryl should be 42° or 43°. Main facets of the pavilion on all other faceting materials should be 40°.

Hardness, Toughness, Ability to Take Polish

Hardness in gemstones is measured by the rather unscientific but very useful Mohs scale of hardness. That this method is practical is demonstrated by the fact that nothing better has ever replaced it since Friedrich Mohs, who died in 1839, invented it. It lists ten minerals according to ascending hardness:

1. Talc	6. Orthoclase
2. Gypsum	7. Quartz
3. Calcite	8. Topaz
4. Fluorite	9. Corundum
5. Apatite	10. Diamond

As far as the gem cutter is concerned, hardness alone, however, does not measure resistance to or ease of cutting. Quartzes are a good example of this. For instance, crystaline quartz, such as amethyst, cuts much easier than cryptocrystaline jasper, which is also quartz.

The more interwoven the crystal structure, the tougher a material, and the less likely it is to splinter. Examples of this, in addition to cryptocrystaline quartzes, are the jades, both jadeite and nephrite, serpentine, and rhodonite.

Ability to take a good polish also is not based on hardness alone. While we can say, as a rule of thumb, that gem materials below hardness 5 are bound to present polishing problems, there are exceptions. For instance, malachite, in spite of its softness (it is 3½–4 on the Mohs scale), takes an easy and brilliant polish. It is fortunate for us that the most easily available, most plentiful stones—the chalcedonies, agates, and jaspers—are often also very beautiful and easy to work with.

Where to Go From Here

After we have mastered the basic techniques of cabochon cutting and faceting, there are many interesting and alluring byways to explore. A book to tell about all these in detail would resemble the Manhattan telephone directory. Let me just enumerate some of them:

Faceting the impossible

Cutting and faceting the odd gemstones

Cutting local gem materials

Intaglio and intarsia work

Cameo cutting

Cutting ashtrays and bowls

Cutting vases

Cutting snuff bottles

Cutting plates and cups

Making beads

Making spheres

Carving in relief and in the round

Finding new methods

Exploring the history of gem cutting

Study of gemmology and mineralogy

Learning how to set your gems in silver and gold

Collecting books on gems and gem cutting

Studying the mechanics of light as related to gem cutting

Glossary

Arbor A bar, shaft, axis, or spindle that supports and is used to revolve cutting, sanding, and polishing attachments.

Arbor Hole The hole in the working appliances that fits on the shaft of lapidary machines.

Bearings Supports in which rotary shafts of lapidary machinery revolve.

Bevel A small rim cut around the bottom of a gemstone, usually at a 45° angle.

Bezel A metal frame used to hold a gem on a piece of jewelry.

Blank A slice of rough gem material sawed or ground to an approximate outline of a projected gemstone.

Bond (of cutting wheel) The material that holds the cutting grit together.

Brilliant A faceted round stone, usually cut with 57 facets.

Bushing The lining of the hole of a grinding wheel — a replaceable lining of a bearing.

Cabochon A gemstone with a smoothly rounded top, usually with one flat surface.

Charge (verb) To impregnate a cutting disc or wheel with a grinding or polishing compound.

Cheating Device A gadget making possible minute sideways movements of a gemstone while mounted in the handpiece of a mechanical faceter.

Chatoyance The phenomenon of a single streak of light appearing on top of a cabochon-cut stone, which moves as the stone is turned in relation to a light source.

Chuck A clamp to hold the dop stick in the handpiece of a faceting device by constriction.

Crown   The part of a faceted stone that will be worn uppermost if the stone is set in jewelry.

Crypto-crystaline (adj.)   Of a mineral, the crystal arrangement of which can only be seen under high magnification.

Cutting (a gemstone)   The operation of grinding it to the desired shape, either on a grinding wheel or a charged lap.

Diamond Wheel Dresser   A steel rod on the tip of which is inserted a piece or pieces of diamond to be used in reconditioning grinding wheels.

Diamond Saw   A round steel disc, the edge of which is impregnated with diamond particles used for sawing gem material.

Dichroism   The property of some gemstones to show two different colors when viewed from different directions.

Dop or Dop Stick   A short rod of wood or metal used to hold a gemstone while it is being worked on.

Dopping Block   A device used aligning two dop sticks for the purpose of correctly mounting or transferring gemstones to be faceted.

Dopping Wax   A compound used to connect a gemstone to a dop stick.

Dressing (a wheel)   To restore a deformed grinding wheel to flatness on its cutting surface.

Emerald Cut   A rectangular stone, the corners of which are ground off so as to form an octagon.

Expanding Drum   A sanding drum on which the sanding cloth is held by the expansion of a specially constructed rubber belt applied to the drum's perimeter.

Facet   A flat polished surface on a transparent gemstone.

Flange   Usually used in pairs. A round disc which is used to hold grinding wheels and saws in place.

Girdle   The line dividing crown and pavilion on a faceted stone.

Girdle Facet   One of a number of small facets adjoining the girdle of a faceted stone, both in crown and pavilion.

Grit   Abrasive powder used in lapidary work, usually silicon carbide.

Grit Size   The size of particles in lapidary powders.

Index (on a faceting device)   The numbered disc which regulates the setting of the stone on the lap.

Jamb Peg   An inverted wooden cone with indentations, fastened next to a faceting lap and used to hold the end of a dop stick in position while cutting.

Lap   A disc of plastic, wood, or metal. Laps are used running horizontally to grind or polish gemstones.

Lapidary   Originally a person working with stones and today meaning only someone working on gemstones. Also used as adjective.

Main (facet)   A principal facet, usually the largest facet on either crown or pavilion.

Matrix   The rock in which a gemstone is imbedded when found.

Mesh Size   A measurement of the size of particles in polishing or grinding powders. Expressed by the number of holes in a square in an imaginary sieve through which the particle would pass.

Micron   One thousandth of a millimeter.

Mud Saw   A disc of mild steel revolving in a mixture of abrasive and water used to cut stone.

Pavilion   The bottom part of faceted stone.

Potch (Australian slang)   Opal without color play.

Preform   A piece of gem material roughly cut to size.

Pulley   A grooved wheel attached to motor and machine shafts. Rubber belts running in the grooves of pulleys transfer power from motor to machine.

Refraction   The property of gemstones to bend rays of light that enter them.

Refractive Index   A listing of varying degrees of deflection from a straight line imparted to a light ray by gem materials.

Rotary Wheel Dresser   An appliance consisting of a cast-iron rod at the tip of which carbon steel wheels are fastened. It is used to recondition grinding wheels.

Rough   Gem material in its natural state.

Sanding   An operation to smooth a gemstone in preparation for polishing. Silicon carbide is used either glued to cloth or paper or applied to other carrier in water solution.

Sanding Cloth   A strip of material to which abrasive is glued on one side.

Set Screw   A screw used to hold in place an appliance on a revolving shaft.

Schiller   A bronzelike luster occurring in some minerals and gemstones.

Shaft   A round steel rod on which rotating machinery revolves.

Slabbing Saw   A large machine that uses a diamond saw to cut large pieces of gem rough into slices.

Splash Pan   A metal pan fastened under grinding and sanding appliances to catch the water used in cooling and lubricating the work.

Star Facet (same as table facet)   One of a number of small facets adjoining the table of a faceted stone.

Step Cuts   A gemstone in which the facets on each side of the gem are parallel to each other.

Table   The flat top surface of a faceted gemstone.

Table Facet   Same as star facet—one of a number of small facets adjoining the table of a faceted stone.

Template   A sheet of plastic or metal with outlines cut into it that serve as patterns to outline the shape of gems.

Tool Rest   A detachable appliance that is fastened in front of grinding wheels to steady objects to be ground or tools which are used in reconditioning the wheels.

Transfer Jig   Same as dopping block.

Trim Saw   A device used to cut slabs of gem material into smaller pieces.

V-dop   A dop stick with a V-shaped notch used to mount elongated stones for faceting.

Wheel   A grinding stone.

Bibliography

Books

BAXTER, WILLIAM T. *Jewelry Gem Cutting and Metalcraft*. New York: Whittlesey House, 1938.

DAKE, DR. H. C., AND PEARL, RICHARD M. *The Art of Gem Cutting*. Portland, Ore.: Mineralogist Publishing Co., 1945.

HOWARD, J. HARRY. *Revised Lapidary Handbook*. Greenville, S.C.: J. Harry Howard, 1946.

KRAUS, EDW. H., AND SLAWSON, CHESTER B. *Gems and Gem Materials*. New York: McGraw-Hill Book Co., 1925.

POUGH, FREDERICK H. *Field Guide to Rocks and Minerals*. Cambridge, Mass.: The Riverside Press, 1953.

QUICK, LELANDE, AND LEIPER, HUGH. *Gemcraft*. Philadelphia, Pa.: Chilton Books, 1959.

SHAW, LOUIS EATON. *Faceting*. Louis E. Shaw, 1961.

SINKANKAS, JOHN. *Gem Cutting*. Princeton, N.J.: D. Van Nostrand Co., Inc., 1955.

SPERISEN, FRANCIS J. *The Art of the Lapidary*. Milwaukee: The Bruce Publishing Co., 1961.

WILLEMS, J. DANIEL. *Gem Cutting*. Peoria, Ill.: The Manual Arts Press, 1948.

Magazines

Gems and Minerals, Mentone, Calif.
Lapidary Journal, San Diego, Calif.
Rock and Gem, Encino, Calif.
Rocks and Minerals, Peekskill, N.Y.

List of Suppliers

It is an impossible task to give a satisfactory list of suppliers in a book of this scope. The 1972 *Rockhound Buyers' Guide* issue of the *Lapidary Journal* lists approximately three thousand dealers catering to the hobby. This list grows by several hundred every year. Many of these dealers operate a mail order business in conjunction with a store. I, therefore, will give only a short list of some of the main manufacturers of equipment, dealers in stones and rough material and other essentials with whom either I or friends and colleagues have done business or who are otherwise known to me by reputation. I can only reiterate my recommendation to obtain the *Guide* and subscribe to the *Lapidary Journal* and one or more of the magazines listed in the bibliography. It is advisable to explore hometown and nearby resources first where things can be seen before buying and help and advice is obtainable. Manufacturers, sometimes, will supply directly to the retail trade, but mostly will refer would-be buyers to the nearest distributor.

BOOKS

Gems and Minerals, Book Dept.
P.O. Box 687
Mentone, Calif. 92359

Lapidary Journal, Book Dept.
P.O. Box 2369
San Diego, Calif. 92112

Peri Lithon Books
P.O. Box 9996
San Diego, Calif. 92109
new, out-of-print, and antiquarian
books on gems and lapidary

Francis Paul Co.
49 Fourth Ave.
Mt. Vernon, N.Y. 10550
back numbers of lapidary magazines

COLLECTING TOOLS

Estwing Manufacturing Co.
2647 Eighth St.
Rockford, Ill. 61101
hammers, chisels, safety goggles

**DIAMOND TOOLS,
LAPS, AND
COMPOUNDS**

Diamond-Pro, Unlimited
P.O. Box 25
Monterey, Calif. 91754
sintered diamond tools

Raytech
P.O. Box 84A
Stafford Springs, Conn. 06076
diamond compounds, Ray-Tilt Gem
Maker, diamond saws

Jack V. Schuller
P.O. Box 420
Park Ridge, Ill. 60068
diamond compounds, diamond laps

**EQUIPMENT
MANUFACTURERS**

Beacon Engineering
Rothsay, Minn. 56579
manufacturers of Beacon Star
grinding units, saws, tumblers,
vibrating laps, and recirculating
pumps

Covington Engineering Corp.
112 First St.
Redlands, Calif. 92373
One of the largest and probably the
oldest firm in the business: grinding
equipment, saws, tumblers, slab
polishers, drills, sphere maker,
lapping units, faceters, tub-type
multipurpose units, grinding wheels,
and saws.

Earth Treasures
Box 1267
Galesburg, Ill. 61401
manufacturers of B and I equipment

Frances Paul Crafts
3–33 La Madera Ave.
El Monte, Calif. 91732
gem drills, bead mills, drilling supplies

Highland Park Manufacturing
Division of Musto Industries
12600 Chadron Ave.
Hawthorne, Calif. 90250
grinding equipment, saws, vibrating
laps, belt sanders, faceting units
(sold only through dealers)

Hillquist
1545 NW Forty-ninth
Seattle, Wash. 98107
one of the oldest firms supplying
equipment to the amateur lapidary

Star Diamond
Division of Craftool Co.
1421 West 240th
Harbor City, Calif. 90710
grinding wheels and equipment, saws,
tumblers, vibrating laps

FACETING MACHINES MANUFACTURERS

Arrow Profile Co.
P.O. Box 38
St. Clair Shores, Mich. 48080
manufacturers of Sapphire Faceter.
Publish monthly a very interesting
four-page information sheet
"The Facetier"

Henry B. Graves Co.
1190 South Old Dixie Highway
Delray Beach, Fla. 33444
manufacturer of Graves Faceter

Lee Lapidaries
3425 W. 117th St.
Cleveland, Ohio 44111
manufacturer of Lee Faceter

M.D.R. Manufacturing Co.
4853 J. W. Jefferson Blvd.
Los Angeles, Calif. 90016
manufacturer of M.D.R. Master II
Faceter. Publisher of a two-volume
compendium of the most popular facet
cuts, with instructions on how to
cut them

O'Brien's
1116 No. Wilcox
Hollywood, Calif. 90038
manufacturers of O'Brien's Faceter,
one of the first firms to make
equipment for the amateur

Stanley Lapidary
503–F South Grand Ave.
Santa Ana, Calif. 92705
manufacturer of Ultra-Tec Faceter

FINDINGS

George Sassen
350 W. Thirty-first St.
New York, N.Y. 10001

Sy Schweitzer & Co.
P.O. Box 431
East Greenwich, R.I. 02818

GEM IDENTIFICATION INSTRUMENTS AND INSTRUCTION

Gemological Institute of America
11940 San Vincente Blvd.
Los Angeles, Calif. 90049

GEM MATERIALS

Alpha Faceting Supply
Box 2133
Bremerton, Wash. 98310
Wide-awake supplier of reasonably
priced faceting rough; also carries
other faceting tools and supplies.

Amber Guild
80–19 Thirty-first Ave.
Jackson Heights, N.Y. 11370
amber for cutting, specimens and
finished jewelry

Australian Gem Trading
294 Little Collins St.
Melbourne
Australia 3000
specialists in Australian opals
and sapphires

Commercial Minerals
22 W. Forty-eighth St.
New York, N.Y. 10036
specialize in fine cut stones, but also
carry some rough materials

Walter E. Johansen
P.O. Box 907
Morgan Hill, Calif. 95037
faceting rough and supplies

Murray American Corp.
15 Commerce St.
Chatham, N.J. 07928
large selection of cabochon and
faceting rough

Parser Mineral Corp.
Box 2076
Danbury, Conn.
fine cabochon and faceting material,
not cheap, but good value

GENERAL LAPIDARY SUPPLIERS
(rough materials, machines, supplies, etc.)

Baskin & Sons, Inc.
732 Union Ave.
Middlesex, N.J. 08846

Gilman's
Hellertown, Pa. 18055

Grieger's, Inc.
1633 East Walnut St.
Pasadena, Calif. 91109

Lapidabrade
8 E. Eagle Road
Havertown, Pa. 19083

Shipleys Mineral House
Gem Village
Bayfield, Colo. 81122

Technicraft Lapidaries
2248 Broadway
New York, N.Y. 10024

Universal Lapidary Division
495 W. John St.
Hicksville, N.Y. 11801

JADE SPECIALISTS

Apex Minerals International
Box 246
Blaine, Wash. 98230

Badger Gem
Route 3, Box 167
Fort Atkinson, Wis.

Bergsten Jade Co.
P.O. Box 2381
Castro Valley, Calif. 94546

House of Jade
P.O. Box 1325
Cambria, Calif. 93428

Jade World
7960 Uva Drive
Redwood Valley, Calif. 95470

Wm. Munz
P.O. Box 639
Nome, Alaska 99762

New World Jade
696 W. First Ave.
Vancouver 9, B.C.
Canada

Index